THE Baffled Parent's

GUIDE TO

Great Soccer

DRILLS

Look for these other Baffled Parent's Guides by Ragged Mountain Press

Coaching Youth Baseball: The Baffled Parent's Guide,
by Bill Thurston

Great Baseball Drills: The Baffled Parent's Guide,
by Jim Garland

Coaching Youth Basketball: The Baffled Parent's Guide,
by David G. Faucher

Great Basketball Drills: The Baffled Parent's Guide,
by Jim Garland

Teaching Kids Golf: The Baffled Parent's Guide,
by Detty Moore

Coaching Boys' Lacrosse: The Baffled Parent's Guide,
by Greg Murrell and Jim Garland

Coaching Youth Soccer: The Baffled Parent's Guide,
by Bobby Clark

Coaching Youth Softball: The Baffled Parent's Guide,
by Jacquie Joseph

THE BAFFLED PARENT'S
GUIDE TO
GREAT SOCCER
DRILLS

Tom Fleck and Ron Quinn

Ragged Mountain Press/McGraw-Hill

Camden, Maine • New York • Chicago • San Francisco • Lisbon • London
Madrid • Mexico City • Milan • New Delhi • San Juan • Seoul • Singapore
Sydney • Toronto

*To my Dad and the entire Fleck family, for all of the support they have
given me throughout my many years in the game of soccer.*
TOM FLECK

*To my wife Celine, for all the years of support in the development of my teaching and
coaching career, and to the boys—Patrick, Brian, and Kevin—for their willingness to
try out new games and activities throughout their childhoods.*
RON QUINN

Ragged Mountain Press

A Division of The **McGraw·Hill** Companies

10 9 8 7 6 5   DOC

Copyright © 2002 Ragged Mountain Press
All rights reserved. The publisher takes no responsibility for the use of any of the materials or
methods described in this book, nor for the products thereof. The name "Ragged Mountain
Press" and the Ragged Mountain Press logo are trademarks of The McGraw-Hill Companies.
Printed in the United States of America.

Library of Congress Cataloging-in-Publication Data
Fleck, Tom.
   The baffled parent's guide to great soccer drills / Tom Fleck and Ron
Quinn.
      p.   cm. — (Baffled parent's guides)
Includes index.
   ISBN 0-07-138488-X
   1. Soccer for children—Training. 2. Soccer for children—Coaching.
I. Quinn, Ron. II. Series.
   GV943.9.T7 F54 2002
   796.334'084'4—dc21   2002004156

Questions regarding the content of this book should be addressed to
Ragged Mountain Press
P.O. Box 220
Camden, ME 04843
www.raggedmountainpress.com

Questions regarding the ordering of this book should be addressed to
The McGraw-Hill Companies
Customer Service Department
P.O. Box 547
Blacklick, OH 43004
Retail customers: 1-800-262-4729
Bookstores: 1-800-722-4726

Illustrations pages 40 (bottom), 45, 50, 51 (2), 52 (top), 54 (2), 57, 60, 65, 66, 72, 79 (bottom),
   83 (bottom), 91, 92 (2), 94, 97, 99–101 (2), 104–7, 113 (bottom), 115, 118, 119, 121, 124–26,
   and 130 by Accurate Art Inc.; pages 44, 46, 49, 53, 59 (bottom), 61 (2), 63, 68–71, 73–76, 82,
   85, 86, 88, 89 (2), 96, 98, 102, 109, 111, 116, 117, 120, 122, and 127 (2) courtesy Ron Quinn
Photography by Greg Rust

Contents

Every player needs a ball.

Introduction

From Parent to Coach

The scene is played over and over throughout the country: Parents take a child to soccer sign-ups and wind up as the head coach or assistant coach. For many, your first reaction may be that you've never played the game, don't know much about it, and don't know what to do next! Some of you may have played in high school or even in college, but the thought of coaching a team of young children may be overwhelming.

Great Soccer Drills: The Baffled Parent's Guide is designed to keep the simple game of soccer "simple" by maintaining a balance among child development, soccer development, and competition. A child-centered approach to coaching and teaching focuses on what happens during the game rather than on the outcome. The book makes a great companion to *Coaching Youth Soccer: The Baffled Parent's Guide*, by Bobby Clark.

The Game/Activity Approach

Children Learn Through Play. Children learn through moving, and they progress in learning as they mature. Today, however, a syndrome known as "The Lost Childhood" has become associated with youth soccer because of the sport's focus on professionalism and business. In their attempts to develop excellence, youth soccer programs are struggling with a staggering 70 percent dropout rate by age 12. Adults often forget that they're teaching young kids and that kids learn and perform as young children. Adults can play children's games but children cannot always play adult games.

The game/activity approach, which is gaining tremendous acceptance in youth soccer, is designed to make *fun*, challenge, creativity, problem solving, and motivation the primary goals of the experience. Through our own observations and through feedback we've received from thousands of coaches in courses and seminars conducted over the past twenty-five years, we have seen this approach succeed. It taps into the essence of children's desires and encourages role-playing, imitation, risk-taking, and lots of action—all attributes that can be accomplished through games.

Therefore, even though the title of this book is *Great Soccer Drills*, you won't find any "drills" here. We strongly believe that traditional drills are too static for most kids, requiring too little decision making and too much waiting in lines. Kids should be involved in activities that are dynamic and exciting, with lots of freedom of movement. The game/activity approach will maintain your team's interest in soccer, and it may also enhance your players' creativity and decision-making skills as well as their physical skills.

How to Use This Book

Great Soccer Drills is designed and organized for both the novice and the experienced coach. Chapter 1, Coaching 101, provides a solid foundation in the purpose of youth soccer and includes sections on understanding the development of players, developing a philosophy of coaching, implementing age-specific coaching, and learning essential coaching concepts.

Chapter 2, Organizing Practices, details the specific ingredients that should be part of every practice session. You will learn how to avoid the three Ls (lines, laps, and lectures), how to keep players active and involve parents, how to get your practices started and keep them flowing, and how to physically and psychologically prepare your players. The chapter also provides answers to many frequently asked questions and includes sample practice plans for each age group.

Chapters 3 to 6 are the heart of this book, with a collection of 125 proven youth soccer games and activities. The games and activities are primarily targeted to boys and girls ages 5 to 12, but many may be applied to soccer players of all ages and ability levels. Chapter 3 describes "ballnastic" warm-up activities that can be used with all age groups. Chapter 4, Body Awareness Games and Activities, takes a "movement education" approach, which emphasizes total body development. These activities use *locomotor movements* (running, jumping, skipping, hopping, and galloping), and *nonlocomotor movements* (bending, stretching, twisting, and curling). They help with the development of *spatial relationships* (near-far, high-low), *movement pathways* (straight, zigzag, bending, round), *movement direction* (right-left, diagonal, forward-backward), and *movement quality* (fast-slow, hard-soft).

Chapter 5, Maze Games and Activities (predominantly chasing and tagging games), presents opportunities for players to move and solve problems in a 360-degree environment. Each activity has an objective, allows for more freedom of movement, and challenges players to expand their field of vision and decision-making skills.

Target Games and Activities in chapter 6 more closely resemble the "real game" and are very effective when a solid foundation has been created through the use of the Body Awareness Games and the Maze Games. Target Games create small-group tactical challenges to take advantage of player maturity and cognitive and mental development.

Youth soccer can be considered the "milk" of youth sport: it is the perfect nutrient for child/player development. Children experience a great deal of running, strength development, eye-foot and eye-hand coordination, spatial awareness, and self-concept and social interaction. Through playing soccer, a child grows in all ways—physical, social, emotional, and mental. However, this does not just happen by itself. It is the responsibility of adults to foster a positive, safe, and enriching youth soccer experience. Offering a very simple approach, this book will be an invaluable tool assisting you in that task. By keeping the experience fun, simple, and rewarding, you can help your players learn lessons they will carry over to life beyond sports.

Who We Are

We've been active in youth soccer for many years and are leading experts and innovators in the area of youth soccer player development. We were instrumental in the design and development of the national and state youth coaching license programs for the U.S. Youth Soccer Association.

Tom holds a doctorate in education from Lehigh University and is a certified elementary educator. He was the director of coaching for the Florida State Youth Association for thirteen years, the first U.S. Youth Soccer Coordinator, general manager of the Philadelphia Fury of the North American Soccer League, and head soccer coach and principal of the Centennial School at Lehigh University. He is the coauthor of the U.S. Youth Soccer Association Parent/Coach Series of coaching booklets. In 1997 he received the first National Soccer Coaches Association of America Bill Jefferies Award for dedication and commitment to youth soccer.

Ron holds a bachelor's degree in health and physical education and master and doctorate degrees in physical education and sport administration. He has been a teacher and coach for twenty-six years at all levels—from elementary school to university physical education and youth to professional coaching. He has written extensively on youth soccer player development and coaching education. Ron is currently an associate professor and director of the sport studies program at Xavier University, where he is also head coach of the women's soccer team.

Small-sided games are the keys to success.

Coaching 101

Understanding the Development of Players

Player development has become the primary goal of several national governing bodies in soccer, including the U.S. Youth Soccer Association (USYSA), American Youth Soccer Organization (AYSO), Soccer Association for Youth (SAY), and others. It has also caught the attention of corporations such as Adidas, Chevrolet, MasterCard, and Pepsi. The flow of dollars and support from these and other organizations to youth soccer and the efforts of countless individuals dedicated to educating coaches are primary reasons why the quality of the game is improving. The purpose of this chapter is to define what is meant by the phrase "player development."

USYSA has coined the phrase "The Game for ALL Kids." The motto of the National Youth License that we have developed is the "Game Within the Child." Both messages imply that the needs of the child playing soccer should be placed above the needs, convenience, and self-interest of adults.

True player development focuses on the development of the individual player, not the development of the team. Although team unity and cohesion is very important, the primary objective should be the positive growth of each player. At the youth level, up to age 14, this should be the only criterion used in designing and running programs. Unfortunately there are all too many instances where this is not the case. We have received calls from parents who indicate that their 6-year-old has been turned off soccer because the coach made the child feel he wasn't any good. (While instructing the National Youth License course, we have encountered numerous examples of youth coaches using coaching methods and training activities that border on abuse.) More recently, one state association was trying to deal with two clubs who wanted to register teams of 3-year-olds! The motivation to register these teams had nothing to do with the kids but was a way to create a family loyalty with the soccer club. We have also witnessed teams of players under age 7 playing eleven-on-eleven! If you've ever seen twenty-two

6- and 7-year-olds playing a game, it probably was not a pretty sight. That number of players is simply overwhelming for that age group, and the safety of each child becomes an issue. These situations have nothing to do with player development.

Player development provides the opportunity for children to play, grow, and mature within an environment that is safe, developmentally appropriate, and growth enhancing. A *safe environment* means that the physical playing area is safe: goals are safely anchored, the field surface is free of glass and rocks, players are aware of traffic patterns and the parking lot, and so on. A safe environment also means that the players are psychologically safe—a player should not be exposed to abusive or denigrating remarks from coaches, teammates, opposing players, or parents. One of the most common fears players have is the fear of failure. If a coach or parent yells at a player for missing an easy goal, the child is less likely to shoot next time. If coaches don't allow players to make mistakes and instead berate them each time they make a mistake, then players will stop taking chances. Once this happens, their development stops, and they are unlikely to become competent, confident, creative players.

A *developmentally appropriate environment* means placing children in situations that are within their physical, intellectual, emotional, and social reach. This does not mean a less challenging environment, but rather one where practice activities are designed to meet players' basic urges to move, instead of standing in lines waiting to dribble through a slalom course of cones. Creating a developmentally appropriate environment also means

Fun and innovation enhance the learning process.

providing instruction players can understand, not placing a 7-year-old at right back and expecting her to stay there and channel forward to the outside. Developmentally appropriate coaching means not yelling at children for making a mistake or making them feel inferior. It means praising all players for the efforts they put forth. If players feel good about what they do, they will continue playing, and their chances of improving increase. If players stop playing, their chances of improving diminish. A child who matures early should not be taken out of her social circle for the sake of a more competitive environment but should have the opportunity to be successful within her own age group and community.

A *growth-enhancing environment* means that children should continue to grow and mature as people through playing soccer. It means that they should seek out challenges and assume some responsibility for their own development through self-organized and self-initiated activities such as pickup games. It does not mean high-intensity training and 2-hour practices for young players or telling players during games when and where to pass or dribble the ball at every instance. It means providing lots of opportunities—through small-sided, appropriate activities—for each child to fully participate.

Valuing and accepting a player development approach is the first step in recognizing your role as a youth soccer coach. The next step is to formulate both a personal and an organizational coaching philosophy. The next sections provide some guidelines to help in this process.

Age-Specific Coaching

The number of children participating in organized sports today is well into the millions. A recent report conducted by the National Sporting Goods Association states that thirteen million players are participating in soccer. The USYSA alone has registered three million players between the ages of 5 and 18.

These numbers have had a definite impact on various segments of our culture. For example, soccer moms have played a role in presidential elections, and large numbers of youth players from all over the world come to the United States to participate in the hundreds of tournaments here.

In addition to the number of youth involved in soccer, tens of thousands of adult volunteers give hours and days of training and administrative, financial, and fan support. These same volunteers contribute an incredible amount of time and effort coaching a most important group of players, those between ages 5 and 12. This group is undergoing tremendous developmental changes during this formative period. This is where an extremely important person comes in: *you, the coach!*

Consequently, you should understand and learn as much as you can about the characteristics of the age group you are coaching. Knowing the game of soccer is only part of the responsibility. The preferred coaching method sweeping the United States is a child-development and game/activity approach. The games and activities found in this book reflect this concept. Allowing kids to play and have fun will help them develop a passion for the game and keep their soccer development moving forward.

One way this can be accomplished is through implementing successful coaching methods. The following concepts are essential for creating a healthy and positive coaching environment.

Essential Concepts: From Theory to Practice

The common notion is that theory has no practical relevance and therefore little real value in coaching. However, the essential concepts (theories) presented here are both realistic and applicable. They should act as a sounding board for every activity or exercise that you have your team do. If you're able to identify the concept behind an activity, you should use that activity. If you can't identify the concept, then you should either change the activity to meet your objective or discard it. The following three essential concepts, although similar, are distinct enough to stand alone.

A quick demonstration helps to get an activity started.

Dr. Muska Mosston's Slanty Line

Dr. Mosston was a pioneer in the identification and development of teaching methods and styles in physical education. He was most known for his book, *Teaching from Command to Discovery*.

The *slanty-line concept* arises from the traditional method of eliminating children as the level of difficulty increases, such as in the game of high-water/low-water played with a rope. In this game, the rope begins on the ground and everyone jumps over it. Then two children raise the rope to a new level, and everyone jumps again. This time, those that are unable to clear the rope are eliminated from the game. This elimination process continues until the best jumper emerges, unfortunately at the expense of everyone else. A typical dodgeball game is played this way. This approach is very counterproductive in the development of children because the individuals who need the activity the most are eliminated earliest.

With Dr. Mosston's approach, the high-water/low-water game is played with a slanted rope. Now, children can run and jump at a level where they feel successful. Children are able to participate at their own ability level. When kids feel comfortable and secure, they will seek out new challenges. Children will not continue in activities where they are continually eliminated or stand in lines to take turns. Given the opportunity, children will seek out challenges and take risks, the very qualities coaches should encourage in their players.

The Everybody's It game (#45) is a good example of this concept. All players have a ball and attempt to tag as many players as possible in the time given. Once tagged, a player is still able to play the game. Whether players earn 5 points or 25 points, all players can play at their own level.

Dr. Mihaly Csikszentmihalyi's Flow Concept

Dr. Csikszentmihalyi, a professor at the University of Chicago, wrote *Beyond Boredom and Anxiety*, in which he introduced the concept of flow.

When you were growing up, how many times were you late for dinner because you got so involved in an activity you lost track of time? Whether you knew it or not, you most likely entered a mental state called *flow*, a period of time where the task at hand matches your ability. Anyone can experience this phenomenon in any activity when those two factors—task and ability—are evenly balanced. This flow concept should be a primary goal of every soccer practice. Try to get your players so involved and engaged in practice that they're surprised when time is up.

When players are not in that flow state, several other emotional and motivational states may occur. If your players' ability is greater than the task or exercise you present, such as slalom dribbling through a series of cones, your players will become bored. It isn't that the players aren't motivated or interested; it's just that the activity isn't sufficiently challenging. Also, when players are asked to perform a task they perceive as beyond their abilities, they'll get frustrated or anxious. Expecting players younger than 8 to perform a *wall pass* (where the receiving player plays the ball back to the passer using only one touch) is unrealistic, since they don't possess the cognitive ability to think in advance of the ball.

All of the small-sided games, if the game is age appropriate, should produce some aspect of the flow concept. Games like Phone Booth Tag (#51), Defrost Tag (#59), Barrel Ball (#72), and Team Knockout (#75), to name a few, will produce high levels of enthusiasm. We have seen a group of 10- to 12-year-old boys and girls play Defrost Tag on a drizzly summer day for an hour. The opportunity to slide in the wet grass probably had a lot to do with it, but they were totally immersed in the activity and didn't know how long they'd been playing.

Dr. Marianne Torbert's Expansion, Equalization, and Interactive Challenges

Dr. Marianne Torbert, director of Temple University's Leonard Gordon Institute for Human Growth through Play, has identified three interrelated concepts that, when applied to play activities, enhance and increase the growth and development of children.

Expanding opportunities for growth experiences. In youth soccer, this would include such things as allowing more turns, increased ball contacts, more equipment (e.g., one ball per person), reducing the downtime between activities, and selecting activities that allow everyone to participate. The Many Goals game (#93) is an example of how you can increase the opportunities players have to improve at playing to a target.

Equalizing challenges so that each player has an equal opportunity for success. This closely relates to the slanty-line and flow concepts. When applied to youth training, it means making a conscious effort to select, design, and provide training sessions that motivate each player, not just the best ones. The Hospital Tag game (#52) is an excellent example of this concept. As the game progresses, some players will be in awkward positions, which may allow less skilled players to tag them. This lets players with different skill levels interact and challenge each other.

Making challenges interactive so that players of different ability levels can participate and interact in a positive, growth-enhancing manner. Since all teams have a wide range of ability levels, it's important that you create an atmosphere in practices that encourages interaction among all players.

The Pac-Man game (#53) demonstrates this concept. As the game progresses, players of lesser ability may become the first additional Pac-Man. As more players have a ball, they receive more opportunities to dribble while, near the end of the game, the faster, more agile players become challenged in a more complex environment.

The application of these essential theoretical concepts is critical to successful player development, which promotes growth instead of restricting it. The activities in this book are based on these concepts while adding the aspects of fun, decision making, creativity, and total involvement.

Developing a Philosophy of Coaching

Developing a coaching philosophy is a crucial step for a beginning or experienced coach. Developing a sound philosophical foundation creates a coaching "conscience," or an internal voice that will help you in difficult situations. If you think this is an unimportant exercise, ask yourself the following: What are my beliefs about cutting players, determining playing time, correcting player mistakes, dealing with parents, promoting player development, experiencing winning and losing, establishing position roles, and so on?

Planning and communication are needed for effective practices.

If you have had to take a coaching action regarding any of the issues just mentioned, that action should have been preceded by conscious decisions on what actions to take in specific situations, so that any decisions made and the subsequent actions taken were based on your beliefs or philosophy. Whether or not you are aware of this philosophy, it still exists. Putting it on paper formalizes and strengthens it. Once you put a philosophy in place, you have a coaching barometer to use as a gauge for making appropriate and consistent decisions.

For example, if you believe that 5- to 8-year-old players should have equal playing time, then your substitution policy will be based on playing time, not the score of the game. One way to accomplish this is to number all of the players on the team. (At this age level, your games should consist of no more than six-on-six with no goalkeeping.) If you have ten players, in the first quarter, players numbered 1 to 6 would play; in the second quarter, players numbered 7 to 10 and 1 and 2 would play; in the third quarter, players numbered 3 to 8 would play; and in the fourth quarter, players numbered 9 and 10 and 1 to 4 would play. The next game, you would start with player number 5. Over the course of the season, players would have equal playing time.

Coaching is both a profession and an ongoing process. To develop your coaching philosophy, answer the following questions.

Beliefs

- Why do I want to be a youth coach?
- Why do we have a youth soccer program?
- What are my responsibilities to each player, to the team, to the community, and to myself?
- How would I define a successful season?

Motivation

- Why am I interested in coaching?
- What do I enjoy most about coaching?
- What do I enjoy least about coaching?

Experiences

- Past: Were my childhood sport experiences enriching or inhibiting? (Either way will influence your beliefs.)
- Present: What am I doing now to improve my coaching?
- Future: What experiences and goals will I pursue to improve my coaching?

Methods

- How would I describe my coaching style? Is it what I want it to be?
- At what point—before, during, and/or after practices—will I involve my players in the decision-making process?

Developing a coaching philosophy allows you to carry out your coaching mission and provide a healthy, safe youth soccer experience. Putting into practice the essential concepts will allow your players to fully participate in practices and games. By using the games and activities in this book, you'll find that your players will begin to develop various game strategies, demonstrate a higher motivation and enthusiasm for practices, and begin to make better decisions during matches. And all of this can be accomplished while having *fun*!

CHAPTER 2

Organizing Practices

The Three Ls: Lines, Laps, and Lectures

"Lines," "laps," and "lectures" are the words youth soccer players like least . . . and older players aren't that fond of them, either.

Lines

Standing in line awaiting a turn should be reserved for the grocery store or mall. Players come to practice to be active, not to stand still. In an activity involving lines, the first few players seem quite satisfied. The first player is dribbling through the cones while numbers two and three are watching. But the rest of the players are well aware that their turn won't be for a while, and it's much more fun to wrestle with the nearest player. Instead of having some players waiting and watching, send all of them off at the same time, each with a ball, so they can all participate. Remember, they come to practice to play, not to wait.

Laps

At some point in our athletic lives, we have all had to run laps. Some coaches give laps as punishment, while other coaches seem to think that laps are the only means to improve fitness. Although we discourage lap running—many of the activities in this book are a great substitute!—if you do have kids run laps, at least give every player a ball and let them dribble as they run around the field.

Incorporating the activities found in this book will provide you with the fitness element that you want and the fun element that your players want. You will be amazed how hard your players will work while also having fun.

One option is to set up an area much like an obstacle course and have the players go through as many of the obstacles as fast as they can in a given time. By adjusting the time allowed, you can probably eliminate the need for warm-up laps. Remember, players come to practice to play.

Players love activities that keep them moving.

As a bonus, they'll be improving their fitness and their technique at the same time.

Activities such as Everybody's It (#45), Pac-Man (#53), and Elbow Tag (#55) are also great to start practices in a fun and physically active manner.

Lectures

It's true—we coaches have a tendency to talk a great deal. Though there's nothing terribly wrong with talking, if you lecture a group of youth players for an extended period of time, they'll usually start to tune you out and not pay attention to what you're saying. Players want to move about and play, so the most effective communication with young players will be brief, clear, and relevant. During the many coaching education programs that we conduct each year, we challenge coaches to get an activity started and the players moving in less than 28 seconds. Try this challenge yourself: Can you give your players brief, clear, concise instructions and get your players moving in 28 seconds or less? We have seen coaches take several minutes to organize and start an activity; by the time the players finally start moving, they don't remember the beginning, which means they ask more questions, requiring more time talking! You certainly want to answer any questions players have, but if you can get the players moving quickly, many of the questions and misunderstandings will resolve themselves.

Involving Players and Parents

Involving Players

Obviously players need to be involved in practices, and this book is designed to provide maximum participation for all players at every practice. However, there are also other ways you can create a sense of ownership and increase motivation in players. In preparing for and implementing practices, you have three opportunities to involve players: preimpact, impact, and postimpact.

Preimpact opportunities involve including players in prepractice decisions. Depending on the age of your players (certainly not before age 9) and your relationship with them, you may wish to seek their input in designing your practices. This can take the form of asking players to identify activities they enjoyed doing in the past, such as an activity they did in a physical education class or some other neighborhood or recess game that could be useful in practices. Involving players here should increase practice concentration and motivation since the players help prepare practices.

Impact opportunities include the players during practice. This is probably the most common technique used, but it's easy to forget how effective it can be. This technique is implemented by asking players questions about the success or failure of an activity or an aspect of an activity. Again, to effectively use this technique, your players will need to be old enough to understand what you're asking and capable of expressing their thoughts clearly. Coaches often assume that they must solve any problems that arise during a practice themselves. But when an activity isn't going as planned, it's often a good idea to ask the players why the activity isn't working. Since the players are performing the activity, it's possible or even likely they may be able to provide some insight regarding any problems. This technique is known as the Socratic method. If the players suggest a particular modification, you should at least try to implement their suggestion, even though you may not think it will work. Successfully creating thinking and motivated players is more about the process than the result. If players are involved in decisions during practice, their interest level and enjoyment will remain high.

Postimpact opportunities involve players in the decision-making process at the end of practices. This may be as simple as asking the players what they thought of the practice, what they enjoyed most or least about the practice, and what they would like to do again. Using this questioning technique at this time either initiates or continues a dialogue with your players. Players will feel that their input is valued, which will continue to develop team unity and individual player motivation.

When using these techniques during any of the impact phases, don't worry that you'll be relinquishing any responsibilities or coaching duties. In fact, you'll probably end up doing more coaching, but interactively, not autocratically, although you should always remain the ultimate decision maker. By using this approach, you'll actually be making more decisions; not only about the format of practices but also those responding to the input provided by your players. One final word of advice: never transmit negative messages to your players. One of your goals should be to create a practice environment where there are no dumb questions and all suggestions are worth discussing.

Involving Parents

Parents can help the team by making phone calls, organizing team drinks and snacks, managing equipment, and organizing fund-raising efforts.

Involving them in practices can be a little more delicate, however. If they have soccer experience and can be impartial (e.g., remove themselves from coaching only their children), then you may find their involvement helpful, especially for practices involving *station work*, where small groups of players rotate to different *stations* (areas of the field) as different skills (dribbling, passing, shooting, etc.) are presented. A parent could be at each station supervising the activity. (They should only supervise, however, and not "coach"; remember, the kids are here to play!)

The key will be to identify specific duties that you want them to perform. Whether a parent should actually play with the team during practice is a safety issue for parents and players. We've seen overexcited parents run over players because they couldn't stop or change direction quickly enough. We would discourage parents from playing with the team unless they have good soccer skills and knowledge, are in good physical condition, and realize that they're there to help all the kids (not just their own) have fun and improve their soccer skills, not to show everyone what good players they are. As in most situations, common sense should prevail so that everyone involved will have a positive experience.

Getting Started

How often have you seen your players standing in front of the goal shooting on the poor kid who happens to go in to get his ball? Generally, they're standing around waiting for you to start practice. What do you think would happen if you never called them in? How long would they just stand there kicking balls at the goal? The point is that we have conditioned our young players to wait for the adult to tell them what to do.

An effective way to help players take more initiative in their own soccer development is to encourage the players to organize themselves in a small-sided game as soon as they arrive at practice. We are not advocating completely eliminating time shooting at the goal but, for example, try encouraging the first two players to put down cones and play one-on-one. Then have them add a player and play two-on-one. As more players arrive and are added, they'll need to decide whether to make the field and/or the goals

Equipment

Fortunately, youth soccer doesn't require lots of (expensive) equipment. Players should be responsible for providing their own "uniform" (shorts, a T-shirt, and footwear with cleats), a soccer ball, and a water bottle.

Each activity in chapters 3 through 6 details the equipment you'll need. Some don't need any. For those that do, you'll usually need one or more balls (you should always bring a few extra, just in case), cones (small and large), flags, and goals (several sizes). Small (3- to 6-inch) and large (6- to 9-inch) cones can generally be used interchangeably to mark the field and playing areas within the field or practice goals (you can also use flags). We've also found small cones (sometimes called *disc cones*) useful in some of our soccer activities (see Elbow Tag, #55). A few of the activities call for swimming pool noodles, which work well and are very safe (see Movable Goal, #64), or scrimmage vests (see Tail Tag, #67).

When you're playing regular games (practice or real), you'll obviously be using the full-size goals on your field. For many of your practice activities, however, you can use cones or flags, as mentioned above, or smaller goals, such as Accu-Goals, more suited to youth players (one good source for these and other equipment is Kwik Goal, www.kwikgoal.com).

Don't forget your whistle and clipboard, a ball pump, the team roster, your practice plan, a first-aid kit (including emergency contact numbers), and ice packs.

larger, or whether to start another small-sided game. Once everyone has arrived for practice, what are they doing? *Playing a game!* Your role now as coach is to observe their play and make mental or written notes on the quality of play, which players emerge as leaders, how players resolve fouls, who takes risks and who plays it safe, and so on. This can be valuable time for the coach as well as the players. After 10 to 15 minutes, call them in, comment on their play, have them begin stretching, and briefly discuss what is planned for practice. Remember: no lectures!

Once practice has begun, your biggest challenge won't be when your players are engaged in an activity but when they're between activities. Unless it's a water break or rest period, this downtime can be very trying. This is when some players' concentration may begin to drift or when some horseplay may occur. To avoid this, reduce the length of time between activities by involving players in picking up cones, flags, and scrimmage vests, and reorganizing the area for the next activity. Also, if you know the next activity in practice will require groups of three, try to end the current activity in some fashion to form groups of three. As an example, if you are playing Math Dribbling (#47), where players must solve a math problem by forming a group of a specific number, your last problem would be two plus one. If you are playing a different activity that doesn't lend itself to such an arrangement, establish a protocol that says whenever you call out a number, players must form that group as quickly as possible. The last group to form will be required to perform some consequence suggested by the team. This does not mean physical punishment but could be something like three quick star jumps or jumping jacks.

Forming Groups

This brings us to another issue regarding practice effectiveness: What's the best way to form groups? How many times have you seen players pick teams, only to see the sad faces on the few players who were picked last? The reality of the situation is that they weren't really picked at all—they were just left over. To create team unity and cohesion, all players must feel they are an important part of the team. The procedure just described does just the opposite. Similarly, games where players are eliminated should themselves be eliminated. It doesn't do anyone any good to have the less skilled players (usually the first ones eliminated) sitting out and the more skilled players still playing! Here are a few alternatives to try.

- During a water break, quickly form groups by randomly passing out vests.
- Form groups by birth months, with January on one side, February on the next, and so on. You could also organize groups by odd and even months, which would take less time.
- Depending on what players are wearing, use dark shirts versus light shirts, solids versus stripes, and so on.
- You may want to try grouping by hobbies or similar tastes or interests, such as those who like country music versus rock, those who like chocolate versus vanilla, and so on.

There are many other creative grouping strategies that you can devise. Most important, it should be done quickly and fairly and no one should be left out. If you're careful about the ways groups are formed, you'll be surprised how quickly team unity develops.

Make organizing groups fun.

Establishing a Practice Plan

Practices should follow a progression from simple to more complex activities, including a warm-up, main practice activities, a small-sided game, and a cooldown. Sample practices are shown on pages 19–30 to help you plan. We've provided sample practices for each age group. You can adjust the times for the individual segments to fit your time schedule and your team's needs.

Body Part Dribbling (#16) and Musical Balls (#66) are good examples of warm-up activities. The important part here is that players are moving for 2 to 3 minutes, and are having fun during the activity, followed by 3 to 5 minutes of stretching. Alternate stretching with movement for 10 to 15 minutes.

During the main activity phase, you may want to concentrate on a particular technique, such as dribbling, but there is also a lot of value in having variety in your practice. During this part, groups are formed and activities become more complex, which may also mean more competitive and/or more cooperative. Some examples are Defrost Tag (#59) and Team in the Middle (#118). Essentially, maze activities along with some target games would dominate this phase, which should last 20 to 30 minutes.

Every practice should include a small-sided game. This doesn't have to mean a full-field scrimmage but would include more gamelike target activities, such as Star Trek (#120) or the Crossing Game (#122). This phase should also last 20 to 30 minutes.

The final phase of the practice involves a cooldown, consisting of stretching and less active individual or group activities. The purpose here is physical as well as psychological. You want players to leave practice feeling good about themselves and their team. Activities such as Zen Dribbling (#19) and Team Knots (#32) are good examples of cooldown activities.

Suggested time limits are given, but you can vary the length of each activity as you see fit. Some teams show a stronger interest in a particular activity; if they like it, go with it. The format and activities listed should serve as guidelines of how a game/activity practice can work. It is also perfectly acceptable to repeat activities in successive practices as well as to choose not to play a particular activity because others are going longer than expected. Particularly with younger players, repeating familiar, fun activities has great value. Additionally, repeating activities with older players allows them to develop game strategies. The general rule of thumb is that the length of practices should not exceed the length of games. If, for example, 5- to 8-year-old players play 12-minute quarters, then their practices should be 45 to 60 minutes. Certainly for this age group, practices should not exceed an hour. Practices for 8- to 10-year-old players should be between 60 and 75 minutes; for 10- to 12-year-old players, 75 to 90 minutes; for players 12 and up, 90 to 105 minutes.

Three Sample Practices for 5- to 8-year-old players
(each practice is 45 to 60 minutes total)

1. Theme: Introduction to the Ball

Warm-up
Every player has a ball. Use the center circle or penalty area, or place cones in a 20-by-30-yard area.

> Body Part Dribbling, #16 (3–5 min.). This age group may have some difficulty with right and left.
>
> Ball Stretching, #4 (2–3 min.). Each player has a ball.
>
> I Can Do Something Without the Ball, Can You?, #13 (3–5 min.). Give each player a turn in the spotlight.
>
> *Water break (2–3 min.)*

Main Activities

> Individual Ball Retrieving, #15 (5–7 min.)
>
> The Glob, #42 (5–7 min.). You may act as the Glob. Remember to move cautiously and don't catch them all at once.
>
> *Water break (2–3 min.)*
>
> Off to the Zoo, #27 (3–5 min.). Use to bring players' activity level down.
>
> Attacking and Defending Gates, #84 (5–7 min.). A great activity to lead players into their game. Focus on individual improvement.
>
> *Water break (5 min.)*

Game (10–12 min.)
Small-sided game of no more than four-on-four with no goalkeepers. You may want to have several balls available to play in when one goes out-of-bounds. You can then play balls into players who are not as active.

Cooldown

> Toes, #17 (2–3 min.)

2. Theme: Introduction to the Ball and Goal

Warm-up
Every player has a ball.

> I Can Do Something with the Ball, Can You?, #14 (3–5 min.)
>
> Ball Stretching, #4 (2–3 min.)

Cross Over, #44 (3–5 min.). Players shouldn't do this too fast.

Water break (2–3 min.)

Main Activities

Movable Goal, #64 (3–5 min.). A pool noodle makes a great moving goal. This is a good way to get parents involved.

Find the Coach, #43 (3–5 min.). You may also want to use parents here.

Water break (5 min.)

Red Light, Green Light, #87 (4–6 min.). A classic.

Balls Galore, #89 (8–10 min.). A good lead-in to your game.

Game (10–12 min.)

Small-sided game of no more than four-on-four with no goalkeepers. This is the fun part; let them play!

Cooldown

Ball Stretching, #4 (2–3 min.)

Edge of the World, #95 (2–3 min.)

3. Theme: Dribbling with a Purpose

This practice will help players make their balls go where they want them to.

Warm-up

Every player has a ball.

Attacking and Defending Gates, #84 (4–6 min.)

Ball Stretching, #4 (2–3 min.)

Water break (2–3 min.)

Main Activities

Snake in the Grass, #25 (4–6 min.). Players really enjoy this; just hope they aren't wearing white T-shirts!

Like Magnets, #41 (4–6 min.). A good activity for introducing changing the direction of the dribble.

Water break (5 min.)

Knock 'em Over, #38 (5–7 min.). Players will like knocking over the cones.

Pick 'em Up, #39 (5–7 min.). Players will like setting them up as well.

Game (10–12 min.).

Small-sided game of no more than four-on-four with no goalkeepers.

Cooldown

Ball Stretching, #4 (2–3 min.)

Zen Dribbling, #19 (2–3 min.). This helps players get a feel for the ball.

Three Sample Practices for 8- to 10-year-old players (each practice is 60 to 75 minutes total)

1. Theme: Introduction to a Partner

Warm-up

Pairs Ball Retrieving, #18 (4–6 min.). One ball per pair; try using birth months to organize pairs (see page 17).

Ball Stretching, #4 (2–3 min.). Players should do this individually.

Main Activities

Math Dribbling, #47 (3–4 min.). Finish with a problem that gets them into twos, and then you will be ready for the next activity.

Peter Pan Dribbling, #48 (4–6 min.)

Water break (2–3 min.)

Pac-Man, #53 (5–7 min.). This moves players back into an individual dribbling activity. Remember to emphasize passing, not shooting.

Bridge Passing, #94 (4–6 min.). Players are in pairs again.

Cooperative Kickball, #56 (10–12 min.). You may want to play at least three innings.

Water break (2–3 min.)

Game (12–15 min.).

Small-sided game of no more than six-on-six with goalkeepers optional.

Cooldown

Ball Stretching, #4 (2–3 min.)

Frantic Ball, #57 (2–3 min.). This isn't as chaotic as it sounds!

2. Theme: Introduction to Small-Group Competition

Warm-up

Various ballnastic activities (4–6 min.). These could include Stationary Ball Taps (#1), Stationary Ball Jumping (#2), Stationary Ball Pickup (#3), Bouncing Body and Ball (#5), and Up and Down (#6), and other activities from chapter 3. Remember to keep these activities fun, not physical chores.

Ball Stretching, #4 (2–3 min.)

Main Activities

Toe Fencing, #20 (2–3 min.)

Water break (2–3 min.)

Tail Tag, #67 (4–6 min.)

Air Ball Scatter, #49 (4–6 min.)

Four-Corner Capture, #100 (6–8 min.)

Water break (2–3 min.)

Game (12–15 min.)

Small-sided game of no more than six-on-six with goalkeepers optional.

Cooldown

Ball Stretching, #4 (2–3 min.)

Soccer Golf, #92 (whatever time you have left). Involve players in creating the course.

3. Theme: Introduction to Dribbling and Playing to Targets

Warm-up

Various ballnastic activities (4–6 min.). These could include Stationary Ball Taps (#1), Stationary Ball Jumping (#2), Stationary Ball Pickup (#3), Bouncing Body and Ball (#5), and Up and Down (#6), and other activities from chapter 3. Keep it fun!

Ball Stretching, #4 (2–3 min.)

Push Up, Pull Down, #21 (2–3 min.)

Main Activities

Fundominals, #24 (2–3 min.). This is also a good exercise for coaches!

Water break (2–3 min.)

Peter Pan Dribbling, #48 (3–5 min.)

Open and Closed Gates, #88 (5–7 min.)

Crows and Cranes, #96 (4–6 min.)

Beehive Breakup, #97 (5–7 min.). Introduces movement off the ball.

Water break (2–3 min.)

Game (12–15 min.)

Small-sided game of no more than six-on-six with goalkeepers optional.

Cooldown

Ball Stretching, #4 (2–3 min.)

Tree Ball, #90 (4 - 6 min.). If you don't have any trees, play Soccer Golf (#91) instead.

Three Sample Practices for 10- to 12-year-old players (each practice is 75 to 90 minutes total)

1. Theme: Working in Small Groups

The activities are becoming more competitive and gamelike, but players continue to work on individual ball skills. Fun is still most important.

Warm-up

Musical Balls, #66 (3–5 min.)

Ball Stretching, #4 (2–3 min.). Stretching now becomes a challenge.

Elbow Tag, #55 (3–5 min.)

Water break (2–3 min.)

Main Activities

Sequence Passing, #76 (4–6 min.). Introduces a passing rhythm. Concentration is a must here.

Keeper's Nest, #60 (3–5 min.)

Keeper's Nest Three-on-One, #61 (3–5 min.)

Meltdown, #78 (8–10 min.)

Water break (5 min.)

Box-on-Box Shooting, #116 (10–12 min.)

Game (12–15 min.)

Small-sided game of no more than eight-on-eight (preferably six-on-six) to two goals.

Cooldown

Soccer Golf, #92 (4–8 min.). Involve players in creating the course.

Ball Stretching, #4 (2–3 min.)

2. Theme: Individual and Small-Group Tactical Problem Solving

Warm-up

Everybody's It, #45 (3–4 min.)

Ball Stretching, #4 (2–3 min.). May want to stretch in pairs.

Hospital Tag, #52 (3–5 min.)

Water break (2–3 min.)

Main Activities

This group of activities is very active; you may not be able to get them all in.

> Phone Booth Tag, #51 (10–12 min.)
>
> Defrost Tag, #59 (10–12 min.). This is lots of fun on a wet field.
>
> *Water break (5 min.)*
>
> Team in the Middle, #118 (10–12 min.)
>
> Star Trek, #120 (10–12 min.)

Game (12–15 min.)

Small-sided game of no more than eight-on-eight (preferably six-on-six) to two goals.

Cooldown

Ball Stretching, #4 (2–3 min.)

Team Knots, #32 (length of time it takes to get unraveled). Players will want to do this several times.

3. Theme: Individual and Group Attacking

This practice will help players think creatively and collectively.

Warm-up

Knockout, #58 (3–5 min.)

Ball Stretching, #4 (2–3 min.)

Creating New Moves, #71 (4–8 min.). How many can your players create?

Water break (2–3 min.)

Main Activities

Attacking and Defending Gates, #84 (8–10 min.)

Soccer Marbles, #65 (5–8 min.)

Team Knockout, #75 (10–15 min.). Let your leaders emerge.

Water break (5 min.)

Game (15–20 min.)

Small-sided game of no more than eight-on-eight (preferably six-on-six) to two goals.

Cooldown

Ball Stretching, #4 (2–3 min.)

Trust Fall, #23 (3–5 min.). Make sure this activity is only done on the grass.

Three Sample Practices for players 12 and up
(each practice is 90 to 105 minutes total)

1. Theme: Group Tactical Play

Fun team competition becomes more intense.

Warm-up

Musical Balls, #66 (3–5 min.). Play continuously with one or two players trying to take a ball. Play 30- to 40-second intervals. Have the players without a ball at the end of the interval perform some simple task.

Ball Stretching, #4 (2–3 min.)

Main Activities

Note that this section now involves fewer activities of longer duration.

Hurricanes and Ladders, #70 (8–10 min.)

Water break (2–3 min.)

Movable Team Goal, #81 (12–15 min.)

Score on the End Line, #102 (12–15 min.)

Water break (2–3 min.)

Game (15–20 min.)

Small-sided game of no more than eight-on-eight to two goals and goalkeepers. As coach, observe more and coach less.

Cooldown

Ball Stretching, #4 (3–5 min.)

Head and Catch, #31 (2–3 min.)

2. Theme: Immediate Support of the Ball

Competition and coordination are key.

Warm-up

One Touch, #79 (3–5 min.). In pairs.

Ball Stretching, #4 (3–4 min.)

Main Activities

Siamese Soccer, #73 (5–8 min.). This is not an easy activity; be patient. Have players remain in pairs for the next activity.

Two-on-One, #105 (10–12 min.)

Soccer Baseball, #109 (12–15 min.). A nice little break that will produce good team spirit.

Water break (2–3 min.)

Throw-Receive-Catch (T-R-C), #115 (12–15 min.)

Game (20–25 min.)

Small-sided game of no more than eight-on-eight to two goals.

Cooldown

Cooldowns are more important now.

Ball Stretching, #4 (3–5 min.)

Standoff, #30 (2–3 min.)

Human Springs, #22 (2–3 min.)

3. Theme: Playing to the feet and moving toward the ball

Warm-up

This age group should start assuming responsibility for warming up for practices.

Triangle Tag, #35 (3–5 min.)

Ball Stretching, #4 (3–5 min.)

Main Activities

Three-on-One Opposite, #77 (5–8 min.). Make sure players stay on the field.

Water break (2–3 min.)

Triangle Goal, #117 (12–15 min.). This is a great transition game.

Barrel Ball, #72 (12–15 min.)

All Up and Back, #121 (12–15 min.). This is your small-sided game with a condition. End practice by removing all conditions and moving right into your eight-on-eight game.

Water break (2–3 min.)

Game (15–20 min.)

Small-sided game of no more than eight-on-eight to two goals.

Cooldown

Ball Stretching, #4 (3–5 min.)

Helicopter, #37 (3–5 min.)

Troubleshooting Chart

Use this chart as a quick way to find suggested solutions for some of the more common problems of youth soccer players.

Note: Keep in mind that the age ranges given here are general guidelines only. All the activities can be modified by varying their length, intensity, and complexity.

Problem	Analysis	Solution
5- to 8-Year-Old Players		
Players bunch around the ball.	This is perfectly natural at this age because they all want the ball.	Make sure each player has a ball. Bunching is OK at this age, but activities 15, 16, 44, and 46 should help.
Players dribble with their heads down.	They need to, or they will lose the ball.	Dribbling is not as easy as it looks. Activities 40, 43, 87, and 88 will challenge them to look around.
Players don't pass the ball.	Why should they? They won't get it back!	Strongly encourage dribbling at this age. Sharing the ball will become an option for this age group. You may want to try activities 18 and 46 using pairs.
Players seem uncoordinated and fall down a lot.	This age group likes falling!	Anatomically, their center of gravity is high, so in essence they are top-heavy. Activities that encourage whole body involvement will help their general motor abilities. Try ballnastic activities 1 and 3–6 and body awareness activities 13–17 and 25–29.
Players 8 and Up		
One or two players seem to dominate the games.	Every team will have players who are ahead of the others developmentally.	This should not be a major concern. Allow them to be successful with their peers. However, activities such as 48, 51, 52, and 97 will provide other players equal chances for success.
A player loses the ball in the game and stops.	This often reflects the types of activities players perform in practice. Are they playing activities in which they are eliminated?	Try activities 53, 56, 58, 65, 93, and 94 to encourage players to immediately chase the ball.
Players aren't able to change their direction of play.	Players will learn how to do this with appropriate practice activities.	This will improve as players improve their ballhandling skills and begin to recognize their other teammates on the field. Try activities 64, 88, 93, 99, and 100.
Players don't pass the ball accurately.	Players aren't swinging their leg in the direction of the ball.	Activities that encourage playing to a target will help. Try activities 49, 50, 51, 53, 59, 65, 69, 76, and 94.
Players have difficulty in one-on-one situations.	This is a confidence as well as a technical issue.	Encourage players to play one-on-one at home and before practice. Try activities 62, 66, 71, and 98.

(continued next page)

Troubleshooting Chart (continued)

Problem	Analysis	Solution
Players 10 and Up		
Players always choose the same partners.	Friendships are important, but so is the need for everyone to feel part of the team.	Activities in which groups are formed randomly and quickly will help create team unity. Try activities 18, 19, 38, 47, 48, and 96.
Players don't stay in position.	They are still learning and want to be around the ball.	Playing in thirds of the field as well as changing the direction of the ball will help. Try activities 75, 101, 102, 118, and 121.
Players avoid heading the ball.	This is natural. Would you want to hit an object with your head?	Fun activities will reduce the fear. Try activities 31, 113, 115, and 122.
Players lack the ability for combination play.	Players are just beginning to recognize how to play collectively.	Implementing small-group activities will provide collective play experience. Try activities 64, 73, 86, 98, 105, and 114.
Players don't seem to know when to shoot.	This common problem is a recognition or timing issue as well as a skill deficiency.	Players love to shoot at the goal so these activities will keep motivation high. Try activities 72, 106, 109, 110, 115, 116, and 119.
Players 12 and Up		
Players don't talk enough during the game.	Some players are very verbal while others are quiet. Once players become more comfortable with themselves and their team members, communication should increase.	Encourage players to call out the name of the player they are passing to. Incorporate this in activities 76, 80, 83, 115, 117, and 120.
The team has trouble with ball possession.	This multifaceted problem could have many sources: poor passing technique, poor movement off the ball, inadequate player communication, and lack of speed in decision making.	Work on improving this at every practice. Try activities 72, 75, 76, 81, 101, 102, 114, and 117–123.
Players don't provide enough support on the ball.	Developing movement to support the ball is difficult to accomplish. At this age, however, players should begin to anticipate or read the game.	Use small-sided games that encourage players to help a teammate and come to meet the ball. Try activities 59, 73, 76, 77, 78, 80, 84, and 114–123.
Players have trouble crossing the ball (missing the goal); when the ball is served from the side, it either goes behind the goal or never reaches it.	Generally this is a strength issue, but it could also be the result of improper technique and timing.	Correct this problem by providing sufficient opportunities for players to serve long balls while in pairs and in small-sided games. Try activities 64, 75, 76, 79–81, 101, 102, 111, 114, and 119–123.

Problem	Analysis	Solution
Players have trouble with first touch when receiving the ball.	Players need to move to the ball and present a flat surface that is perpendicular to the flight of the ball.	Players can work on this skill every day through activities and exercises that involve receiving ground and air balls in small and large spaces. Try activities 36, 75–77, 80, 83, 103, 104, 112, 114, 115, and 118.
Players keep getting knocked off the ball and are running out of breath in the second half of the game.	In practices, use intervals of activity and rest to improve player fitness.	One way to get the most out of activities is to apply the following three principles: (1) once an activity starts, everyone is moving; (2) never let the ball stop rolling; and (3) attempt to take every ball out of the air (don't let it bounce). All of the activities promote fitness, but those that have a stronger fitness base include 1–12, 20, 21, 24, 35, 77, 82, 112, and all small-sided and small-group games.

Questions and Answers

Coaches often ask us questions about youth soccer situations. The following deal with some of the common issues coaches have.

Q. What should I tell parents when they want to move their son or daughter to an older age group?

A. Several factors should be considered here. Is it really what the player wants to do, and if so, why? Is the player mature enough and physically ready? Has the parent considered the long-term implications for the player? Common sense dictates that a youth player should not play up more than 2 years. Even then, the player must be well prepared in case she doesn't fit on the team successfully and is forced to play down the next season. We believe that a conservative approach should be taken for players under age 12. Prior to their secondary growth spurt, remaining with their peer group has many advantages. What's wrong with a child being successful with her own age group?

Q. What should I tell players about playing indoor soccer during their outdoor season?

A. Consider two important factors: players can burn out if they play too much soccer, and most indoor games are played with the walls in-bounds (players can play the ball off the walls). From a player development perspective, playing indoors where the walls are out-of-bounds will encourage more opportunities for ball control and possession. Playing indoors can be a great deal of fun for young players, but having distinct breaks between seasons will allow them to reenergize.

Q. How bad is it for young players to head the ball in soccer?

A. Many questions have been raised on this issue. To date, most of the head injuries to young players have been the result of a collision between two players, with the field surface, or with a goal post. Research has indicated no adverse effects from heading the ball. However, note that most young players don't head the ball—they duck. This is OK, and it isn't necessary to spend a great deal of time with heading. Exercises with heading should emphasize striking the ball with the forehead.

Q. What should I tell a 12-year-old girl who wants to play on an all-boys' team?

A. If she is properly prepared for the transition, it could prove beneficial. The operative word in the previous sentence is "prepared." Her preparation should include physical and definitely psychological discussions since she will be subjected to various kinds of heckling from opposing players and sometimes her own teammates. Reassurance from parents, players, and her coach will help a great deal.

Q. One of my players always gets dropped off late for practice. How do I handle this situation?

A. Talk to the player's parent to find out why the player is always late. Perhaps the player can carpool with someone else, or maybe the parent doesn't realize the importance of getting to practice on time.

CHAPTER 3

Ballnastic Warm-Up Activities

Ballnastics are a series of body and ball developmental exercises. The underlying principle is to create a wide range of movement challenges that include strength building, coordination, and social as well as competitive and cooperative exercises. At practices, they can be done individually, in pairs, or in small groups. Players can also do them at home.

Ballnastic activities are appropriate for all age groups as long as the challenges are within the players' capabilities. Younger players do these for the development of hand-eye and foot-eye coordination and overall body control. Older players do these for the development of strength, local muscle endurance, and foot speed.

These exercises should be presented in a fun, challenging fashion. Younger children will fall and giggle, but don't interpret this as a lack of interest. The rest period between each set of exercises should be at least as long as it takes to perform the exercise. Depending on the intensity of the exercise, a 1:2 or 1:3 activity-to-rest ratio may be more appropriate. For example, a 1:2 activity-to-rest ratio is one where 1-minute activity periods alternate with 2-minute rest periods. The key is that an all-out effort is made during the active periods.

Please note that this activity list is not comprehensive; the range of movement challenges that can be presented and created is limitless. Remember to keep the movements safe and within the ability range of the age group you are coaching.

Individual Ballnastic Activities

1. Stationary Ball Taps

Purpose: To develop foot quickness.

Number of Players: All
Equipment: 1 ball per player
Time: 20 to 30 seconds for each interval
Ages: All

Place a ball in front of each player. On your signal, each player touches the ball with the sole of the foot, alternating feet as fast as possible. Younger players (ages 5 to 7) will have difficulty coordinating the right and left feet and will need more time. Older players (ages 8 and up) will have a body rhythm and will be able to develop faster foot movement.

Always have the players do this more than once, challenging them to improve on their last try.

Variation: Have players use only the soles of their feet to move the balls forward, backward, and sideways. The task can be for either time or a fixed distance.

2. Stationary Ball Jumping

Purpose: To develop foot quickness and local muscle endurance.

Number of Players: All
Equipment: 1 ball per player
Time: 20 to 30 seconds for each interval
Ages: 10 and up

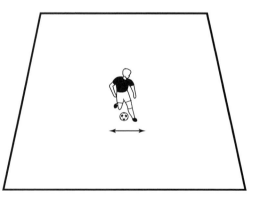

With their feet together, have players jump forward and backward over the balls. How many jumps can they do in the time allotted?

Variation: Have the players jump side to side.

3. Stationary Ball Pickup

Purpose: To develop leg strength and flexibility.	**Number of Players:** All **Equipment:** 1 ball per player **Time:** 20 to 30 seconds for each interval **Ages:** All

Begin with a ball between each player's feet. On your signal, players see how many times they can lift the balls with their feet and catch them with their hands. The goal is to improve their personal best.

4. Ball Stretching

Purpose: To prepare players for practice. (*Safety note*: It is important to have your players move first before stretching. Stretching should also be slow and static.)	**Number of Players:** All **Equipment:** 1 ball per player **Time:** 20 to 30 seconds for each interval **Ages:** All

First, have players stand with their legs apart and have them roll the balls with their hands through their legs eight times in a figure eight. Next, have them place one leg forward and one leg behind them and roll the balls with their hands around their front foot ten times. Then switch feet.

Now, with the players sitting down, legs together and straight out in front of them, have them roll the balls to their toes without letting go and with both hands on the ball. Can they go past their toes? They should not take their fingers off the ball. Have them hold this stretch for 30 seconds. Finally, with the players sitting with their legs straight but apart in a V shape, have them roll the balls along the outside of one leg, around that foot, over to the other foot, and behind their backs. Can they do this five times? Reverse the direction.

5. Bouncing Body and Ball

Purpose: To develop a body rhythm.

Number of Players: All
Equipment: 1 ball per player
Time: 20 to 30 seconds for each interval
Ages: All

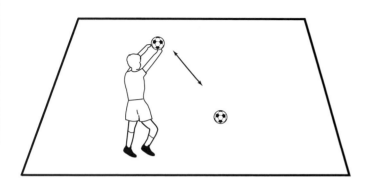

With the balls in their hands, have the players attempt to bounce the balls using both hands while jumping at the same time. The goal is to jump and bounce in unison. See how many jumps and bounces the players can do in the time allotted.

Variation: Have the players jump up and, with both hands, throw the balls to the ground as hard as they can to get the highest bounce possible. They should then jump up and catch the balls. Or, while jumping and bouncing, have the players bounce the balls through their legs, turn, and catch it.

6. Up and Down

Purpose: To develop body quickness and leg strength.

Number of Players: All
Equipment: 1 ball per player
Time: 20 to 30 seconds for each interval
Ages: All

First, have the players lie on their backs and see how many times in a row they can toss the balls straight up and catch them. Next, how many times in a row can they toss the balls straight up, sit up, and catch them? Next, with players lying on their backs or sitting up, how many times in a row can they toss the balls straight up, stand up, and catch them either before they hit the ground or after one bounce?

Now have players stand. First, have them toss the balls high in the air and jump up and catch them while they're in the air. Next, have them toss the balls in the air, quickly sit down and get back up, and catch the balls before they hit the ground or after one bounce. Finally, have them toss the balls in the air, do a forward roll, and get up and catch the balls before they hit the ground or after one bounce.

Safety note: Make sure your players can do a forward roll correctly.

7. Abs, Abs, and More Abs

Purpose: To develop abdominal strength and quickness.

Number of Players: All
Equipment: 1 ball per player
Time: 20 to 60 seconds for each interval
Ages: 10 and up

First, have the players sit and place the balls between their feet. With their knees bent and their arms folded across their chests, how many sit-ups can they do in 30 seconds? 45 seconds? 60 seconds?

Next, have the players sit up with their feet off the ground and the balls in their hands and weave the balls between their legs in a figure eight.

Then, have the players sit with their legs slightly bent and the balls between their feet. Can they move their legs back and forth over the balls without letting their feet hit the ground? Have them do this for 20, 25, and 30 seconds.

8. Arms, Arms, and More Arms

Purpose: To develop upper-body strength.

Number of Players: All
Equipment: 1 ball per player
Time: 20 to 60 seconds for each interval
Ages: All

How many push-ups can your players do in 20 seconds? 30 seconds?

Have the players assume a push-up position and place their hands on the balls. How many push-ups can they do on the balls?

Have the players put the balls under their chests. How many push-ups can they do around the balls (without touching the balls)?

Have all the players try doing the push-ups with their legs fully extended and toes touching the ground. If any players are having difficulty, have them do modified push-ups by bending their legs and having their knees touch the ground.

Competitive and Cooperative Exercises in Pairs

9. Over and Under

Purpose: To work together in pairs while stretching and moving.

Number of Players: All, in pairs
Equipment: 1 ball per pair
Time: 20 to 30 seconds for each interval
Ages: 8 and up

Have the pairs stand back to back with some space between them and with one ball. One player hands the ball to the other player over his head with hands outstretched; then they both bend forward, and the player who received the ball hands it back under—between his legs. The ball should be handed, not tossed. Continue this over-and-under sequence for 20 to 30 seconds.

10. Side to Side

Purpose: To work together in pairs while stretching and moving.

Number of Players: All, in pairs
Equipment: 1 ball per pair
Time: 20 to 30 seconds for each interval
Ages: 8 and up

Have each pair of players stand back to back with some space between them and with one ball. Both players twist to the same side and exchange the ball. They then twist to the other side and hand the ball back. Have them continue in this side-to-side sequence for 20 to 30 seconds.

Variation: Have each pair stand back to back with some space between them and with one ball. Both players twist to their right (an opposite or full-twist motion) and exchange the ball. They then twist to the left and hand the ball back. Have them continue in a right-to-left sequence for 20 to 30 seconds.

11. Balls Away

Purpose: To develop the ability to track a flighted ball, bring an air ball under control, and dribble with speed.

Number of Players: All, in pairs
Equipment: 1 ball per player
Time: 8 to 10 minutes
Ages: 10 and up

In a large area, have the players send their balls high into the air either by foot or hand. The object is to recover the balls with their feet in less than four bounces and return them to their starting point by dribbling with speed. The partner who returns her ball in four bounces or less earns 1 point. The first player in each pair to reach 5 points wins.

If you believe that your younger players can do this activity, allow them to have more bounces at the beginning.

12. Ball Wrestling

Purpose: To develop upper-body strength and tenacity.

Number of Players: All, in pairs
Equipment: 1 ball per pair
Time: 20 to 30 seconds for each interval
Ages: 10 and up

Have each pair of players grasp the ball firmly. On your signal, the players try to wrestle the ball free from their partners. The player who gets the ball free wins the point. Play the best of three or five tries and then switch partners.

Body Awareness Games and Activities

Body awareness activities are those in which players experience moving with and without the ball. The goals are to create a better understanding of the many different ways the body moves (bending, stretching, rolling, twisting), and knowledge of body parts (knee, elbow) and directions (left foot, right foot). We believe coaches have a responsibility to develop players' entire bodies: feet, legs, trunk, hands, arms, and the brain. This in turn develops more physically and mentally competent individuals.

Individual Body Awareness

13. I Can Do Something Without the Ball, Can You?

Purpose: To get players more familiar with their bodies without the ball and with contributing to the practice session with creative suggestions.	**Number of Players:** All **Equipment:** None **Time:** 5 to 10 minutes **Ages:** 5 to 8

Challenge your players by saying, "I can do something without the ball, can you?," and starting to skip. Players should copy you, skipping in a random fashion within the defined area. Then repeat the challenge and demonstrate another movement (hopping, running and clapping, walking backward, etc.). After the players get the hang of it, then ask them, "Who can show us something you can do without the ball?" (Be ready for anything!)

14. I Can Do Something with the Ball, Can You?

Purpose: To get players more familiar with their bodies and the ball and with contributing to the practice session with creative suggestions.	**Number of Players:** All **Equipment:** 1 ball per player **Time:** 5 to 10 minutes **Ages:** 5 to 8

Your challenges can be similar to the previous activity except this time conduct them with a ball. Again, after the players get the hang of it, ask them, "Who can show us something you can do with the ball?" (Again, be ready for anything!)

15. Individual Ball Retrieving

Purpose: To encourage quick thinking and problem solving while allowing players to imitate other players.	**Number of Players:** All **Equipment:** 1 ball per player **Time:** 5 to 10 minutes **Ages:** 5 to 8

Have the players hand you their balls one at a time. You then toss each ball away, and players must retrieve their balls as quickly as possible and bring them back any way they want. Encourage players to bring the balls back a different way each time. Examples include carrying the ball back with one or both hands, holding it on the head, placing it between the knees, or carrying it with the elbows.

After several return opportunities, call out a number between 1 and 15 as each player gives you the ball. Once you've tossed it away, the player's challenge is to bring the ball back while touching it that number of times.

16. Body Part Dribbling

Purpose: To improve dribbling skills in a confined area, reaction time, listening skills, and knowledge of body parts.

Number of Players: All
Equipment: 1 ball per player
Time: 3 to 5 minutes
Ages: 5 to 8

Place players in a random formation within a confined space (such as the center circle). Have players dribble and control their balls without touching any other players. While they are moving, call out a body part (elbow, foot, knee, stomach). The players must immediately stop the balls with that body part. If you choose, the last person to react may have to do a small task, such as three ball taps or some fun exercise. The task should not be considered a punishment, and the remaining players should return to dribbling while the player is completing the task.

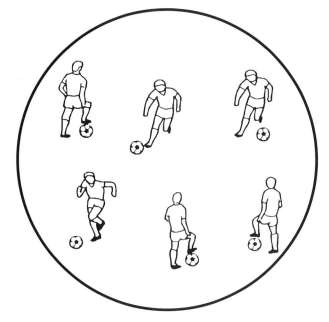

17. Toes

Purpose: To stretch muscles in a fun and creative manner while allowing players to interpret and solve problems in their own way.	**Number of Players:** All **Equipment:** None **Time:** 3 to 5 minutes **Ages:** 5 to 8

Have the players sit down and hold their toes. Their legs should be straight out in front of them with their right hands touching right feet and left hands touching left feet. Through all of the instructions, the players must not let go of their toes. Suggested challenges include the following.

- Can they make one leg longer than the other? Switch legs.
- How wide can they stretch their legs?
- How small can they make themselves?
- How large can they make themselves?
- How narrow can they make themselves?
- Can they get their feet higher than their heads?
- Can they place their feet behind their heads?
- Can they stand up and walk without letting go of their toes?

Let players get creative and interpret the challenges however they want. This can be used as a warm-up or cooldown activity.

Body Awareness in Pairs

18. Pairs Ball Retrieving

Purpose: To introduce the concept of working in pairs to solve spatial problems through short passes and to encourage players to play to their feet, which will improve passing accuracy.	**Number of Players:** All, in pairs **Equipment:** 1 ball per pair **Time:** 5 to 10 minutes **Ages:** 7 to 10

Begin by calling out a number between 2 and 15 to each pair and tossing the ball away. Each pair must retrieve the ball as quickly as possible in the number of passes called out. The final pass should be back to you.

19. Zen Dribbling

Purpose: To develop a greater sense of ball awareness.	**Number of Players:** All, in pairs **Equipment:** 1 ball per pair **Time:** 2 to 3 minutes **Ages:** All

Have each pair hold hands, with one player ready to dribble. The player with the ball closes her eyes and tries to dribble while her partner begins to walk around the field leading her by the hand. Her partner's role to is make sure she is safe and doesn't dribble off the field or into another pair.

20. Toe Fencing

Purpose: To develop foot quickness.	**Number of Players:** All, in pairs **Equipment:** None **Time:** 30 to 60 seconds **Ages:** 8 and up

Have the partners face each other with their arms on each others' shoulders and without a ball. On your signal, players try to touch their partner's toes without their own toes being touched. Score 1 point for each touch. No kicking is allowed.

21. Push Up, Pull Down

Purpose: To improve reaction time and shoulder strength.

Number of Players: All, in pairs
Equipment: None
Time: Best of 3 or 5 tries
Ages: 11 and up

Have partners face each other in a push-up position. On your signal, players try to pull each other down at the wrist without slapping at each other's arms.

Safety note: Strongly encourage players to grab their partner's wrist from the inside and pull out. Be extremely careful that players do not strike the elbow from the outside, since the arm does not bend that way.

22. Human Springs

Purpose: To promote cooperation and trust.

Number of Players: All, in pairs
Equipment: None
Time: Until players fall down
Ages: 11 and up

Have partners stand facing each other with their hands up and touching only each other's palms. Both players lean in and then push off and "spring" back. Have them repeat until they get into a rhythm. Players then take a step backward, getting a little farther apart, and do the same springing motion. Make sure they meet each other in the middle at the same time. They should continue to get farther apart until they fall down.

23. Trust Fall

Purpose: To develop a sense of trust and cooperation between teammates.

Number of Players: All, in pairs
Equipment: None
Time: Until each player has had a turn
Ages: 11 and up

Have partners stand one behind the other. The player in front should close his eyes and put his arms out slightly. Staying as stiff as possible, the player falls backward, and his partner catches him under the arms. Once a catch is made, the catching partner takes one step back, and the other partner falls back again. This time, he falls a little farther and must trust his teammate to catch him.

Emphasize that players must not drop anyone. Partners should be of similar weight and strength so they will be able to catch each other. Reverse roles after a few tries.

24. Fundominals

Purpose: To strengthen abdominal muscles.

Number of Players: All, in pairs
Equipment: None
Time: 30 to 60 seconds for each interval
Ages: 9 and up

Have each pair sit facing each other with knees bent and feet off the ground. Players try to maintain a balanced position while they try to push their partner off balance using only their feet. Contact is made only through the feet, and hands and feet may not touch the ground. A point is scored if a player can push her partner off balance so that the partner's back touches the ground.

Small-Group Body Awareness

25. Snake in the Grass

Purpose: To improve running, jumping, agility, and balance.

Number of Players: All
Equipment: 4 cones
Time: Until all players are snakes
Ages: 5 to 8

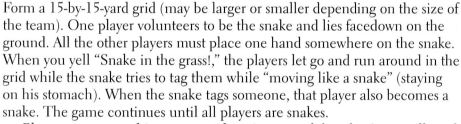

Form a 15-by-15-yard grid (may be larger or smaller depending on the size of the team). One player volunteers to be the snake and lies facedown on the ground. All the other players must place one hand somewhere on the snake. When you yell "Snake in the grass!," the players let go and run around in the grid while the snake tries to tag them while "moving like a snake" (staying on his stomach). When the snake tags someone, that player also becomes a snake. The game continues until all players are snakes.

Players can run and jump to avoid getting tagged, but they're not allowed to step on a snake! This is a good warm-up activity or early-season ice-breaker.

26. Human Obstacle Course

Purpose: A creative dribbling activity that is a great icebreaker for younger players.

Number of Players: All

Equipment: None at first, then add 1 ball per player

Time: Until each player has completed the obstacle course at least once

Ages: 5 to 8

Players should do this activity without the ball at first. Ask one player to get into a position that she can stay in comfortably, such as standing with her legs apart, rolled up in a ball, or on her hands and knees. The next player then goes around, through, under, or over the first player and then gets into a different position. The third player goes through the first two and takes yet another position. This continues until all players are part of the obstacle course. At this point, have the first players go again so they can go through a complete course.

After all players have gone through, add one ball per player. Now each player must dribble through the course. The course continues to evolve with each player creating a new shape once that player has completed the course.

27. Off to the Zoo

Purpose: To improve body control, agility, creativity, balance, and imagination.

Number of Players: All
Equipment: None at first, then add 1 ball per player
Time: 5 to 10 minutes
Ages: 5 to 8

First, have the players move around in the center circle without a ball imitating an animal that you call out. You should name a variety of animals, which will change the players' actions from crawling to standing to flying to swimming movements.

Once the players understand the activity, give each player a ball and see how well the players deal with making flying or swimming motions with a ball.

28. Walk the Line

Purpose: To improve balance.

Number of Players: All
Equipment: None
Time: 3 to 5 minutes
Ages: 5 to 8

Using the lines on the soccer field, players walk the line without "falling off." The penalty box (the 18-yard box) and center circle are good areas for this activity.

29. Sitting Soles

Purpose: To improve eye-foot coordination.

Number of Players: All, in groups of 3 or 4
Equipment: 1 ball per group
Time: 5 to 8 minutes
Ages: 5 to 8

Have each group of three or four sit in a small circle. They must keep their ball moving using only the bottoms of their feet. Players may also try to juggle the ball with their feet from that position. If the ball goes out of the circle, the whole group must move like a big crab (they must remain sitting and use only their hands and feet to move) to get it.

30. Standoff

Purpose: To improve balance.

Number of Players: All, in pairs
Equipment: None
Time: 3 to 5 minutes
Ages: 10 and up

Have partners stand facing each other approximately 2 feet apart, and with their feet close together (but not touching). Players raise their hands with palms facing their partner and attempt to push each other off balance. The first person to move her feet loses the round. Players can only touch each other with their hands. This is a game of strength as well as skill.

31. Head and Catch

Purpose: To develop quick and accurate reponses to ball movements.	**Number of Players:** All, in pairs **Equipment:** 1 ball per pair **Time:** 1-minute intervals **Ages:** 10 and up

Have partners stand facing each other approximately 2 yards apart. The player with the ball tosses it in the direction of his partner's head and calls out either "Head" or "Catch." The player receiving the ball reacts accordingly by either catching the ball or heading it back. Repeat this process rapidly for about a minute, then have players switch roles. Players should toss the ball at the same height each time.

This is a fun, quick-thinking activity that provides the opportunity to head the ball without really thinking about the act of heading.

Variation: Once both players are familiar with the exercise, see how quickly they respond when they do the opposite of what was called out.

32. Team Knots

Purpose: To improve patience, leadership, and problem-solving skills.	**Number of Players:** All, in groups of 6 to 10 **Equipment:** None **Time:** Until the knot is untangled **Ages:** 8 and up

Have players stand in a circle with their shoulders touching. On your signal, players close their eyes and reach into the circle with both hands to grab someone else's hands. Players must grip hands only. When the players open their eyes, they should have a human knot. Players then must communicate and solve the problem of untangling themselves without letting go of the hands they are holding. This is a great way to end a practice.

33. Lightning Fast

Purpose: To improve body speed, agility, reaction time, creativity, and dribbling with speed and control.

Number of Players: All
Equipment: 1 ball per player
Time: 3 to 5 minutes
Ages: All

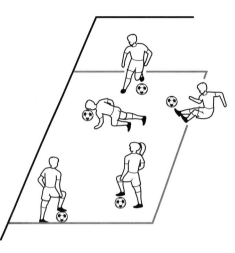

Have each player dribble a ball inside the penalty box. When you call out a number, the players must touch their balls with that many different body parts. For example, if you call "four," each player must quickly touch the ball with four different body parts, such as the hand, toes, heel, and knee.

34. Circle Tag

Purpose: To develop a competitive and cooperative atmosphere among players.

Number of Players: All, in groups of 8 to 11 (group size can vary according to number of players at practice)
Equipment: None
Time: Until a player is tagged (game can be played for 3 to 5 minutes)
Ages: 10 and up

Have each group of players join hands and form a circle around one player who stands as still as a statue in the middle of the circle. The circle players begin pulling and tugging in an attempt to pull someone into the circle to touch the "statue." The player who touches the statue becomes the new statue. Make sure players do not pull too hard or make quick, forceful movements.

35. Triangle Tag

Purpose: To develop quick, deceptive, lateral, movements.

Number of Players: All, in groups of 4
Equipment: None
Time: Until each player has been both a target and a chaser
Ages: 8 and up

Have three players in each group form a triangle by placing their arms on one another's shoulders. The fourth player stands outside the triangle. The triangle players select one of themselves to be the target. The player on the outside attempts to tag the target while the triangle players move from side to side to protect the target. The triangle players do not run but stay in a limited space. Play continues until the target is tagged or everyone is tired. Make sure that everyone has the opportunity to be a target and a chaser. This is a good quickness and fitness activity as well as a lot of fun.

36. Jiggle, Jangle, Juggle

Purpose: To improve ball control, agility, concentration, visual focus, and touch.

Number of Players: All
Equipment: 1 ball per player
Time: 8 to 10 minutes
Ages: 8 and up

Give the players plenty of space, and have them juggle the balls (keep them in the air) using their head, shoulders, thighs, and feet for 60 to 90 seconds. Then call a freeze, and ask players how many touches they had. During this 2- to 3-minute break, challenge players to beat their previous score. For younger players, allow the balls to bounce once between touches, if needed. Players should be encouraged to do this activity on their own outside of practice.

37. Helicopter

Purpose: To develop team unity and cohesion.

Number of Players: 8 to 10
Equipment: None
Time: Until each player has a turn in the middle
Ages: 11 and up

Have players sit in a circle with their legs together and facing in, like spokes on a wheel. One player stands in the middle with his arms crossed or at his sides, making himself as stiff as possible. All the sitting players hold their arms up. The player in the middle falls back onto the outstretched arms of the sitting players. The sitting players pass the player around the circle. The sitting player who lets the middle player fall down becomes the new player in the middle.

Make sure the player in the middle remains stiff and the sitting players keep their hands up or in front of them.

CHAPTER 5

Maze Games and Activities

In maze activities, players must navigate in mostly a 360-degree environment to solve various spatial problems. The purpose of these activities is to provide opportunities for developing players to move in a variety of ways, to solve movement problems individually and collectively, and to experience using the ball in lots of different situations.

38. Knock 'em Over

Purpose: To develop the ability to dribble with the head up.

Number of Players: All
Equipment: 1 ball per player, 15 to 20 large cones
Time: 5 minutes (or according to players' development level)
Ages: 5 to 8

Players dribble in an appropriately sized area trying to knock over as many cones in 10 to 20 seconds as they can. Set the time according to the players' level of development.

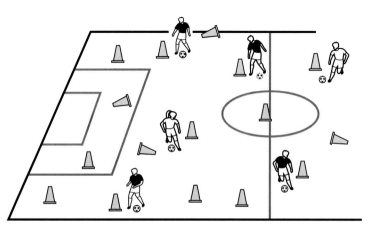

MAZE GAMES AND ACTIVITIES

39. Pick 'em Up

Purpose: To develop the ability to dribble with the head up while maintaining body motion, control, and balance.

Number of Players: All
Equipment: 1 ball per player, 15 to 20 small or large cones
Time: 5 to 7 minutes
Ages: 5 to 8

Have the players dribble in the same size area as the previous activity. Challenge them to move with speed, maintaining balance while putting the cones in an upright position. The game can be played by teams or by individual players.

40. Follow the Leader

Purpose: To develop coordination and balance with a ball.

Number of Players: All
Equipment: 1 ball per player, 1 ball for coach
Time: 6 to 8 minutes
Ages: 5 to 8

Have the players follow you while dribbling in an appropriately sized area. Along the way, hop on one foot, skip, walk as though on a tightrope, sit down, and so on, while keeping your ball moving with various parts of your body. After the players have imitated you for a time, call upon various players to be the leader.

41. Like Magnets

Purpose: To develop the skill of changing direction while dribbling.

Number of Players: All
Equipment: 1 ball per player
Time: 3 to 5 minutes
Ages: 5 to 8

In a confined area, such as the center circle or penalty box, have players dribble while pretending they are magnets. Whenever they come close to another player, they must immediately "repel" by changing direction and sprinting away for 3 to 5 yards.

42. The Glob

Purpose: To develop the ability to change direction.	**Number of Players:** All **Equipment:** None at first, then add 1 ball per player **Time:** 5 to 10 minutes **Ages:** 5 to 8

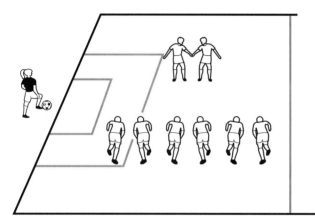

Position all of the players but two on one end line of a half field or on one side of a 30-by-40-yard grid. You and the two other players join hands and start as the Glob. On your signal, players run and try to get to the other side or an end line without being tagged by the Glob. Players tagged by the Glob leave the game, perform four alternating ball touches with their feet, and then reenter the game. After a few rounds, select two new players to join you as the Glob. Play until every player who wants a turn as part of the Glob has one.

Variation: Give each player a ball and have players dribble while trying to avoid the Glob.

43. Find the Coach

Purpose: To encourage players to look up while dribbling.	**Number of Players:** All **Equipment:** 1 ball per player **Time:** 3 to 5 minutes **Ages:** 5 to 8

Players hand you their balls one at a time, and you throw each ball in different directions. Players run to retrieve the balls and must dribble them back to you with their feet. You do not remain stationary, however, but move all over the activity area. This means players must dribble with speed and with their eyes up to see where you are. This improves players' decision making.

44. Cross Over

Purpose: To improve dribbling skills while avoiding contact with other players.

Number of Players: All
Equipment: 1 ball per player
Time: 3 to 5 minutes
Ages: 5 to 8

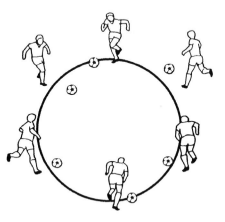

Have players begin dribbling in the same direction along the outside of the center circle. On your signal, players attempt to cross through the circle without touching each other.

If the group is large, have players count off by twos. Then when you call "1" or "2," players with those numbers quickly turn and dribble across the circle without touching other players.

45. Everybody's It

Purpose: To encourage an attack mentality, shielding, and using all surfaces of the ball.

Number of Players: All
Equipment: 1 ball per player
Time: 1- to 2-minute intervals
Ages: All

Have each player dribble within the center circle and attempt to tag other players while maintaining control of the ball. One point is awarded for each tag.

46. Gates

Purpose: To improve decision-making skills by dribbling to many targets while changing direction.

Number of Players: All
Equipment: 1 ball per player, several cones or Kwik Goal Accu-Goals
Time: 5 to 10 minutes
Ages: 5 to 8

Place cones 3 yards apart as small goals or "gates" (or use Accu-Goals; see sidebar page 16) randomly throughout a 30-by-30-yard grid. On your signal, the players dribble their balls through as many gates as possible in 1 minute. At the end, ask them how many gates they dribbled through. Then repeat, and challenge them to improve on that number.

47. Math Dribbling

Purpose: To develop dribbling skills in a confined area while changing direction and speed.

Number of Players: All
Equipment: 1 ball per player
Time: 3 to 5 minutes
Ages: All

Begin by having players dribble in a confined area without touching each other. Then call out a math problem (appropriate for the age level). The players must immediately solve the problem and demonstrate the answer by forming a group with the correct number of players.

For example, if you call out "2 + 2," players should quickly form groups of four. The last group to form, or a group that has the wrong number of players, must perform some small physical task, such as three sit-ups. The key here is that players must form groups as quickly as possible, so the players closest to each other will form groups, instead of searching out their buddies.

For a little fun, try calling out 1×1, and see what happens. And, if your next activity involves pairs or groups of three, make your last math problem in this activity $1 + 1$ or $1 + 2$.

48. Peter Pan Dribbling

Purpose: To develop dribbling skills with the head up while maintaining ball control.

Number of Players: All, in pairs
Equipment: 1 ball per player
Time: 1-minute intervals
Ages: 8 and up

One partner in each pair holds a ball. Have the other partner dribble the ball, following the ball-holding partner and attempting to stay within that partner's shadow. Players switch roles after 1 minute.

49. Air Ball Scatter

Purpose: To develop sprinting and encourage quick thinking.

Number of Players: All
Equipment: 1 ball
Time: 3 to 5 minutes
Ages: 8 and up

Have players form a circle with one player, who has the ball, in the middle. The player in the middle throws the ball high in the air, and the other players scatter. While the ball is in the air, the thrower calls the name of one of the running players. The thrower then joins the running players. The player whose name was called must get to the ball as quickly as possible. If the player catches the ball before it hits the ground, the player throws it up in the air and calls another player's name. If the ball hits the ground, the player retrieves it and yells "Freeze!," and all of the running players must freeze. The player who called the freeze then gets one shot (with the feet) at any one of the frozen players. (Remember to emphasize accuracy, not power.) If a player is hit, that player assumes the thrower position and play resumes. If no one is hit by the shot, then the shooter must perform a reasonable consequence. The players can make up some sort of fun consequence for the thrower, but it must be safe. Play then resumes, and continues until time is up.

50. Gauntlet

Purpose: To develop short passing skills by striking other players with the ball.

Number of Players: All, in two teams of equal number
Equipment: 1 ball per player on team A
Time: 3 to 5 minutes
Ages: 8 and up

Have team A form a circle around team B. Team A players pass their balls with their feet, which helps promote passing accuracy. Team B players try not to get hit, which requires swift body movement and 360-degree visual awareness. Once a team B player is hit while running, the player can then only walk. Once a walking player is hit, the player must then crawl. If a crawling player is hit, the player continues to crawl until time is up; no one is eliminated. Make sure team A players are making passes to hit the team B players, not taking hard shots at them.

At the end of 60 to 90 seconds, call a freeze and tally the score for team A: team B players who are still running earn team A 1 point, those who are walking earn them 3 points, and those who are crawling earn them 5 points. Then the teams switch roles, so team A is on the inside and team B is on the outside. Team B now tries to get more points than team A, which means they must hit more team A players more often.

Variation: Have team A players stay on outside of circle.

51. Phone Booth Tag

Purpose: To improve body speed and reaction time, and encourage dribbling with speed (for variation).

Number of Players: All
Equipment: 1 ball per player (for variation), 12 to 16 cones
Time: 3 to 5 minutes
Ages: 8 and up

Form three or four squares ("phone booths") by placing the cones (four for each square) about a yard apart from one another. Place the phone booths randomly in the designated area. Select one or two players to be It, and chase the other players. Each phone booth acts as a safe base for the players who run into it. However, there can be no more than two players in a safe base at one time. This means that if there are two players in a phone booth and another player enters, the player who has been there the longest must leave or become It. A tagged player also becomes It.

Variation: Give each player, except those who are It, a ball. Players now must dribble the balls when they're moving and going into and out of the phone booths. If a phone booth has too many players, the player who has been there the longest must give her ball to one of the players who is It. This also occurs if a dribbling player gets tagged outside of a phone booth.

52. Hospital Tag

Purpose: To improve dribbling while off balance or in an awkward position.

Number of Players: All
Equipment: 1 ball per player
Time: 3 to 5 minutes
Ages: 8 and up

This is similar to the previous activity, but here, each time a player is tagged, the spot that was touched is considered "injured." The player must hold that spot while continuing to dribble. The second time a player is tagged, the player must also hold that new spot without letting go of the first spot. Players continue to dribble and tag other players as best as they can. The third time a player is tagged, the player goes to the area designated as the "hospital" and must complete some activity, such as ten alternating ball touches with the feet. Upon completion, the player is completely "healed" and returns to the game.

The value of this activity is that although less-skilled players may go to the hospital first, they'll soon be able to rejoin the game. This provides a sense of being part of the group regardless of ability level.

53. Pac-Man

Purpose: To develop the ability to hit a moving target while dribbling.

Number of Players: All
Equipment: 1 ball per player, 4 cones
Time: 3 to 5 minutes
Ages: 8 and up

Create a 20-by-20-yard grid. You can vary the size of the grid depending on the number of players and their ages. Select one or two players to be Pac-Men and give each one a ball. The other players do not start with balls but run freely within the designated area. The player(s) with the balls dribbles and attempts to hit the other players below the waist by passing the ball at them; emphasize passing rather than shooting. When players are hit below the waist, they become a Pac-Man, collect a ball, and help hit other players. Play continues until all players are Pac-Men.

If a player is hit early, he has the opportunity to dribble longer. If a player manages to avoid getting hit until near the end, his challenge greatly increases.

54. Knee Tag

Purpose: To keep control of the ball while trying to tag an opponent's knees.

Number of Players: All
Equipment: 1 ball per player
Time: 3 to 5 minutes
Ages: 8 and up

This is similar to Everybody's It (#45), except players collect points by tagging other players on the knee. This activity forces players to lower their center of gravity, expand peripheral vision, and increase leg strength from the flexed position of the legs.

55. Elbow Tag

Purpose: To teach anticipation and quick thinking.

Number of Players: All, in pairs
Equipment: Several small cones or small soft foam balls
Time: 5 to 10 minutes
Ages: 8 and up

Have players stand with the elbows of one arm hooked with their partner's. The other hand is on the waist with the elbow bent. You break apart one or two pairs and give one or two of the players a disc cone (see sidebar page 16) or ball. The players with the cones or balls chase the other player and try to tag the player with the cone or ball (it may not be thrown). If a player is tagged, the cone or ball is dropped, and the player who was tagged picks up the

cone or ball and becomes the chaser. A chaser can be "safe" by hooking up with a player who has an elbow that is not hooked. Once this occurs, the player on the other side must leave and is now being chased by the chaser.

Once players get the hang of it, break up more pairs so you have more chasers and runners. Players chasing can tag anyone who is not safely linked to an elbow. Continue adding chasers and runners until the game completely falls apart from sheer fun and chaos.

56. Cooperative Kickball

Purpose: To develop cooperation and competition.

Number of Players: All, in two teams of equal number
Equipment: 1 ball, 4 cones
Time: 10 to 20 minutes
Ages: 8 and up

This is played like a regular kickball game (with cones as bases), except for the following rule changes.

- Don't keep track of outs; the inning is over when everyone has kicked.
- All teammates of the player who fields the ball (hands may be used to field the ball) quickly run to that player and form a line behind him. The player with the ball hands the ball over his head to the player behind him, who then bends over and hands the ball to the next player through his legs. Proceed in this over-and-under fashion until the ball gets to the end of the line. The last player to receive the ball runs to the front and yells "Stop!" If the fielding team is able to yell "Stop!" before the kicker runs across home plate, the kicker is out; if not, the kicker scores a run. (Catching a kicked ball before it hits the ground or tagging the kicker with the ball do not count as outs.)
- The kicking player must run around and touch all of the bases. The player cannot stop at any of the bases; the run ends with either an out or a run scored.

Variation: If your players' skill level allows, restrict the fielding players to using only soccer skills when receiving the ball (use of hands is not allowed).

57. Frantic Ball

Purpose: To encourage very quick one-touch passing.

Number of Players: All, in two teams of equal number
Equipment: At least 1 ball per player on team B
Time: 3 to 5 minutes
Ages: 8 and up

Have team A form a circle approximately 10 yards in diameter around team B. The team B players each have a ball at their feet. When you call out "Frantic ball!," team B players begin passing their balls within the circle. They can touch a ball only once before they must pass another ball.

This activity is similar to a team juggle, where all the balls must be rolling at all times. Team A players can act as a wall and are allowed to one-touch balls back into the circle. Team A players cannot stop the balls and should try not to let any balls leave the circle. You or a designated player should watch for balls that have stopped rolling inside the circle. Every time you see a still ball, call out "Frantic!" or some other fun word until you have called out the word ten times. Time the exercise to see how long it takes to get to ten; then have the teams switch roles.

58. Knockout

Purpose: To learn to maintain possession of the ball while trying to kick an opponent's ball away.

Number of Players: All
Equipment: 1 ball per player
Time: 1- to 2-minute intervals
Ages: 8 and up

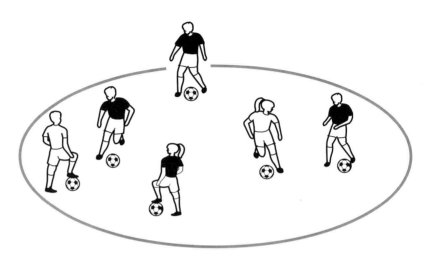

Position the players randomly in a circle. Each player dribbles while trying to kick another player's ball out of the circle. When a player's ball is kicked away and she catches up to it before it stops, she can rejoin the game. If the ball has stopped, the player must perform four to ten alternating ball taps (touching the top of the ball with the sole of the foot) before rejoining the game.

59. Defrost Tag

Purpose: To encourage quick, accurate short passes and improve group communication.

Number of Players: All, in two teams of equal number
Equipment: 1 ball per player on team A, 4 cones
Time: 10 to 20 minutes
Ages: 8 and up

Create a 20-by-30-yard grid. Place team B inside the grid without balls. Team A starts outside the grid. On your signal, team A players dribble into the grid and attempt to hit team B players with short passes. Encourage team B players to run, jump, and dodge to avoid being hit. Players who are hit are frozen and must stand with their legs apart and hands on their hips. Frozen players can be unfrozen when a teammate crawls through their legs. However, as long as any part of the crawling player's body is still under the frozen player, both players are safe and a ball cannot be played. Only when the player crawls completely through can the frozen player become unfrozen and both players actively rejoin the game.

Time how long it takes team A to freeze all the team B players, or use a fixed time limit in which you count the number of frozen players at the given time. Then switch roles and see if team B can improve on team A's result.

60. Keeper's Nest

Purpose: To encourage offensive players to work together to distract defensive players.

Number of Players: All, in groups of 4
Equipment: 1 ball per group
Time: 3 to 5 minutes
Ages: 8 and up

One player (the keeper) in each group guards but cannot touch the ball. (The ball may also be placed on a disc cone; see sidebar page 16.) The objective is for the other three players in each group to get the ball away from the keeper without being tagged and frozen by the keeper. The keeper's goal is to freeze all three players before they get the ball. A frozen player remains still at the point of contact and may count slowly to ten (e.g., 1001, 1002, 1003 . . . 1010). Players trying to take the ball may use their feet or hands. Continue until all players have been the keeper.

Safety note: Keepers should not swing their arms wildly in an attempt to tag the other players.

61. Keeper's Nest Three-on-One

Purpose: To develop passing angles while passing through a goal.

Number of Players: All, in groups of 4
Equipment: 1 ball and 3 cones per group
Time: 5 to 10 minutes
Ages: 8 and up

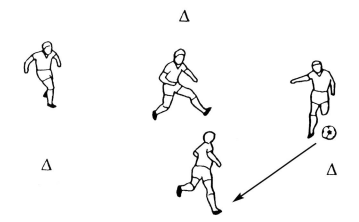

Each group places their cones 5 to 8 yards apart to form a triangle. Each cone represents a goal. One player from each group (the keeper) stands inside the triangle and may not leave it. The three players on the outside try to pass the ball through one side of the triangle and out through another. The keeper tries to keep the ball from penetrating the triangle from a pass, while the three players attempt to pass the ball between them and move the keeper out of position so that the ball can be played through two sides.

The three players don't need to play the ball through the triangle every time; possession can also be maintained by passing the ball around the triangle. However, only balls that go through the triangle earn points; the passer receives 1 point for each succesful pass through the triangle. If the keeper intercepts the ball, the player who played the ball last becomes the new keeper.

62. Draw

Purpose: To improve foot quickness and reaction time.

Number of Players: All, in pairs
Equipment: 1 ball per pair
Time: 1 to 2 minutes
Ages: 8 and up

Have partners face each other with the ball between them at a distance of one step from the ball. Both players stand with their feet parallel, so that a straight line is across their toes. When you or a designated player calls out "Draw!," each partner tries to be the first to pull the ball back with the sole of his foot. You may want to complete several rounds, or the best of a series.

You can have a little fun by calling out words that are similar to "draw," such as "drum," "dragon," and so on. This will force the players to concentrate on the word you're calling out. This activity is a good way to start small-sided games.

Variation: Play one-on-one immediately following the draw. The player with the ball at the end of 30 seconds receives 1 point. Play several rounds.

63. Chain Tag

Purpose: To develop communication and coordination skills.

Number of Players: All
Equipment: None
Time: 3 to 5 minutes
Ages: 10 and up

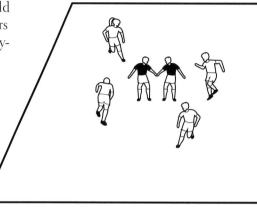

Position all but two players on the end line of a half field or on one side of a 30-by-40-yard grid. Select two players to be It, and have them join hands. On your signal, players attempt to run across the field without being tagged by the two players holding hands. Players tagged by the chain join it. Once all players are across the area, they turn and run back. When the chain grows to six players, break it into two chains of three. Play continues until all players are part of a chain.

Safety note: This is a very fun game, but it is *not* a "crack-the-whip" activity. Participating players should be old enough to understand that someone could get seriously injured if the rules aren't followed. Emphasize that players should work together and should not "whip" the last person off the chain.

64. Movable Goal

Purpose: To develop scoring ability by attempting to score on a moving goal.

Number of Players: All
Equipment: 1 ball per player, 1 or 2 swimming pool noodles
Time: 5 to 10 minutes
Ages: All

Choose two players to hold each end of a pool noodle (these work well and are very safe). The players holding the noodle become the goal and run around on half the field while all the other players, each with a ball, try to dribble and score on the moving goal. Play 2- or 3-minute intervals and see how many goals can be scored either individually or collectively.

Variation: Play using pairs.

65. Soccer Marbles

Purpose: To improve passing accuracy by hitting a moving target.

Number of Players: All, in pairs
Equipment: 1 ball per player
Time: 5 to 8 minutes
Ages: 8 and up

Position players in a large open space, or you can use a full field. One player in each pair passes his ball 5 to 10 yards away. The second player then attempts to pass his ball to hit the first ball while it is either still or moving. For a hit, score 1 point. For a miss, the moment the passed ball goes completely past the target ball, the other player may play his ball. Thus, players learn to immediately chase their balls each time they play them. Players can pass only their own ball.

If a player hits a ball and scores a point but his ball is only inches away from the ball he hit, allow him to restart the game with a new pass away from the area to provide more of a challenge.

66. Musical Balls

Purpose: To develop the ability to identify and sprint to a loose ball.

Number of Players: All
Equipment: 1 ball per player
Time: 3 to 5 minutes
Ages: All

This activity is played like musical chairs. Players dribble their balls within the defined area (center circle, etc.). On the whistle or your chosen signal, all players must leave their balls and find a new ball to dribble. With children older than 7, have the last player to get to her ball perform some small task, such as six alternating touches of the ball, then begin dribbling again. This is a great warm-up activity and helps younger players part with their balls.

Variation: For players 8 and older, take away the ball from the last player to reach her ball. Continue play and take away a new ball with each change. Continue to remove up to three or four balls, depending on the size of the group. When you're ready to end the activity, gradually readd the balls so everyone ends the game with a ball.

67. Tail Tag

Purpose: To develop balance, quick direction changes, and creative decision making (scheming).

Number of Players: All
Equipment: 1 scrimmage vest or bib per player
Time: 1 or 2 minutes
Ages: 9 and up

Have each player tuck a scrimmage vest into the back of their shorts. On your signal, players see how many "tails" they can gather. Players who lose their tails continue to play. The player with the most tails wins the round.

This makes a good warm-up activity.

68. Train Tag

Purpose: To develop balance, quick direction changes, and creative decision making (scheming).

Number of Players: All, in groups of 3
Equipment: 1 vest per group
Time: 1 to 2 minutes
Ages: 9 and up

Have each group form a "train": two players place their hands on the player in front of them, so there is an engine (the first player), a passenger car (the second player), and a caboose (the third player). The cabooses tuck the vest in the back of their shorts. The engines try to grab the vests from the other cabooses.

This is a good warm-up activity and encourages small-group interaction.

69. Dynamic Passing

Purpose: To improve concentration, working as a group, and one-touch passing.

Number of Players: 4 to 8
Equipment: 1 ball
Time: 3 to 5 minutes
Ages: 10 and up

Position the players in two lines 10 to 12 yards apart. The lines should face each other. The first player in line 1 passes to the first player in line 2, then runs to the end of line 2. Repeat until all players in line 1 have made a pass. Using one-touch passing, players must maintain the straight shape of their line. If a ball is played wide or short of the receiving player, the entire line must make the adjustment made by the receiving player.

Variation: This activity also may be done using two-handed chest passes to improve passing accuracy, quickness off the ball, and sprinting short distances.

70. Hurricanes and Ladders

Purpose: To improve group cooperation, eye-hand coordination, sprinting, and flexibility.

Number of Players: 6 to 9, in two groups
Equipment: 1 ball
Time: 3 to 5 minutes
Ages: 9 and up

Have one group act as the "hurricane" and the other as the "ladder." The ladder group forms a straight line. You toss out the ball, and the whole ladder group runs to retrieve it. Then they alternate passing the ball overhead and between their legs to each player in the group. Meanwhile, the hurricane group forms a huddle, except for one player who runs around the group as many times as she can.

When the last player in the ladder group gets the ball, she must run to the front of the line and yell "Stop!" The running hurricane player must stop at that point. Then ask how many circles the running hurricane player made. Players then switch roles and repeat the activity. The goal is to see which group makes more circles around their "hurricane."

71. Creating New Moves

Purpose: To develop problem-solving skills by encouraging players to create new dribbling moves using ball or body feints.

Number of Players: All, in pairs
Equipment: 1 ball per pair
Time: 10 minutes
Ages: 9 and up

Body fakes and ball fakes enable players to get behind and past defenders. A *body fake* is a feint or fake that requires some type of body movement prior to moving the ball, such as starting to go right and then making a quick switch and going left. A *ball fake* is a feint or fake in which the initial feinting movement is done with the ball, such as pushing the ball right, then quickly pulling it back and going left.

Have players pair off and try to create two body fakes and two ball fakes. Challenge them to see how many different moves they can come up with. One player acts as a defender, giving passive resistance so the offensive player has the opportunity to work on the movement. After about 10 minutes, bring the players together and ask them to demonstrate their moves. You may also want to see who comes up with the most creative but sensible move. Remind the players that the objective in using any deceptive dribbling move is to get behind and past the defender. The move is a part of the process, not an end in itself.

72. Barrel Ball

Purpose: To build teamwork and encourage problem solving, quick thinking, and creativity.

Number of Players: All, in two teams
Equipment: 1 ball, 1 round trash barrel
Time: Unlimited
Ages: 9 and up

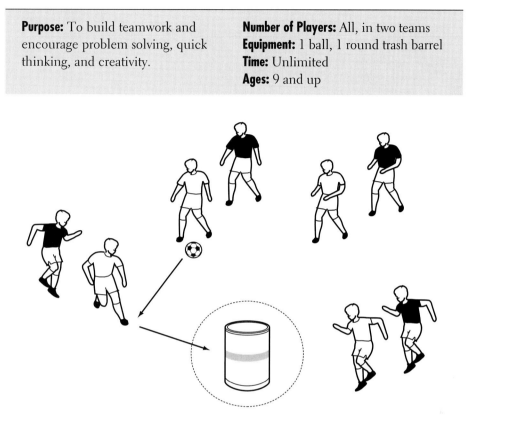

Teams can have the same or a different number of players. Place the barrel in the middle of the field. This game is played like any small-sided game except that both teams are attacking and defending the barrel. The last player to touch the ball before it hits the barrel scores a goal for his team. No one may touch the barrel! Players call all fouls and resolve all disputes. This is a great activity to start or end a practice.

Variation: Draw or form a 5- to 10-yard circle around the barrel. This becomes a free zone that will force players to defend the circle. No one is permitted in the circle.

MAZE GAMES AND ACTIVITIES

73. Siamese Soccer

Purpose: To improve passing accuracy and cooperation by working in pairs to hit a moving target, and to introduce the concept of a wall pass.

Number of Players: All, in pairs
Equipment: 1 ball per running pair(s)
Time: 3 to 5 minutes
Ages: 10 and up

This activity is similar to the Pac-Man game (#53) except that one or two pairs begin with the ball. All other pairs join hands and run in a confined area to avoid being hit by a pass. The pair or pairs of players with the ball(s) dribble and pass between themselves, attempting to pass and hit other pairs in the area. When a running pair is hit, they break apart, collect a ball, and become part of the pairs who are passing the balls. Play continues until all running pairs have become passing pairs.

Variation: To introduce the concept of a *wall pass*, a pass in which the receiving player plays the ball back to the passer using only one touch, add the condition that for a hit to count, the hit must come from a one-touch pass.

74. Ready, Get Set, Burst!

Purpose: To develop the ability to dribble at full speed with the head up and to find safe spaces to dribble.

Number of Players: All
Equipment: 1 ball per player
Time: 5 to 6 minutes
Ages: 10 and up

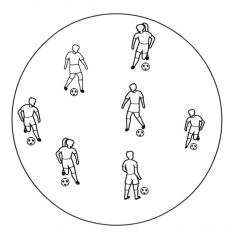

Have all of the players dribble in the center circle. On your signal, the players must burst into an open space while continuing to dribble their balls without colliding into another player. If a collision does happen, both players must stop and do five ball taps on their balls to reenter the game.

75. Team Knockout

Purpose: To introduce the concepts of possession and team play.

Number of Players: 12 to 18, in two teams of 6 or 9

Equipment: 6 to 9 balls for team B

Time: Depends on ability and interest level

Ages: 10 and up

Position the two teams on a half field. Team B is on the field and each player has a ball. Team A is along the sidelines without balls. On your signal, you start the clock and team A runs onto the field and attempts to kick all the balls off the field. Stop the clock when the last ball is kicked off the field. Team B players who have had their balls kicked off the field are now able to help other team members by getting into position to receive a pass. The objective here is to see how long team B can keep at least one ball in play and/or to see how quickly team A can kick all the balls off the field. Once the last ball is kicked out of play, the roles reverse and team A tries to beat team B's time.

This is an excellent activity for improving communication and the concept of team possession through a fun and competitive small-sided game.

76. Sequence Passing

Purpose: To create a passing rhythm by following a specific passing sequence.

Number of Players: All, in groups of 5 to 7
Equipment: 1 ball per group
Time: 5 to 7 minutes
Ages: 10 and up

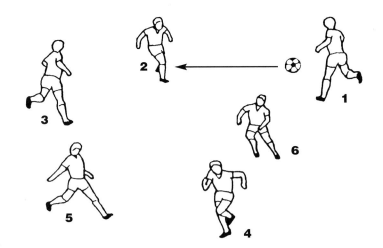

In a general space, randomly number players in sequence starting with number 1. The activity starts with player 1 in possession of the ball. All players move and run without the ball within the space provided. Player 1 then passes to player 2 and runs off the ball. Player 2 receives the ball and looks for player 3. As player 2 is receiving the ball, player 3 should begin moving into position to receive the ball from player 2. This sequence continues with the last person playing the ball to player 1. After players pass a ball, they need to move into a space away from the next pass.

This activity gets everyone involved and all the players moving. Encourage playing to the feet and sprinting after a ball is played.

Variation: Once players are into a passing rhythm, add a second ball and challenge them to not be the person with two balls. This encourages speed of preparation and play.

77. Three-on-One Opposite

Purpose: To develop dribbling, passing, and receiving and encourage communication and creativity.

Number of Players: All, in groups of 4
Equipment: 1 ball per group
Time: 5 to 10 minutes
Ages: 10 and up

Have the groups play in an area up to one quarter of the field. Players play three-on-one keep-away for a few minutes. If the player in the middle of each group gets the ball, the player who made the pass goes in the middle. Now for the fun part: players now play opposites, meaning that the player in the middle, instead of trying to get the ball, now must tag a player who does not have the ball. A player in possession of the ball cannot be tagged. The tagged player becomes the new player in the middle.

78. Meltdown

Purpose: To encourage cooperation and teamwork.

Number of Players: Three teams of 4 to 6 players each

Equipment: 2 to 3 balls for the attacking team, 4 cones

Time: 5 to 10 minutes

Ages: 10 and up

Create a 30-by-30-yard grid. Combine two of the teams to make one defending team. Give the balls to the remaining team, the attacking team. The defending team players run freely within the space. The attacking team players dribble and pass between one another while trying to hit the defenders below the waist with the ball. Attackers may decide to hit off a dribble or a pass. Once defenders are hit, they are frozen and stand with their hands on top of their heads. The attacking team tries to freeze everyone. A frozen player is unfrozen when two defenders surround the player by joining hands and moving up and down around the frozen player yelling "Meltdown!" Defenders trying to melt a frozen player can be hit with the ball. If the attacking team doesn't freeze everyone within 5 minutes, stop the game. Now the attacking team becomes part of the defending team, and half of the defending team becomes the attacking team.

Variation: Add a little twist by allowing the defending team to also be on the offensive. Now the defending team can cause a meltdown of their own if they can join hands with any number of players and surround an attacker and yell "Meltdown!" The ball is then taken out of play. The goal for the defending team is to eliminate all of the balls.

79. One Touch

Purpose: To improve one-touch passing to a partner.

Number of Players: All, in pairs
Equipment: 1 ball per pair
Time: 5 to 10 minutes
Ages: 10 and up

Position the pairs of players in an open or confined area suited to the players' ability level (larger for older players, smaller for younger ones). At a distance of 15 to 25 yards, partners send passes to each other that must be played back using only one touch. The objective is to play without miskicking the ball or using more than one touch. A point is awarded to the partner of the player who misplays the ball. Play either until someone reaches 5 points, or like the basketball games of "horse" or "pig," in which you call out a letter of "horse" or "pig" each time a player misplays the ball. The first player who misplays the ball enough times to spell the word loses that round, and a point is awarded to their partner.

This activity forces players to solve technical problems quickly and strike balls at different angles, speeds, and body positions.

80. Short-Short-Long

Purpose: To introduce the concept of changing the point of attack.

Number of Players: All, in groups of 5 to 8
Equipment: 1 ball per group
Time: 5 to 15 minutes
Ages: 10 and up

Position the groups of players on a half field. Each group passes the ball using a passing pattern of two short passes followed by a long pass. This can be used as a warm-up activity.

Variation: Play a small-sided game for possession or to goal with each team following the short-short-long pattern either for a point or before they can go to goal.

MAZE GAMES AND ACTIVITIES

81. Movable Team Goal

Purpose: To score on a moving goal using team play.

Number of Players: Two teams of 6 to 8 players each
Equipment: 1 ball per player, 1 swimming pool noodle per team
Time: 10 to 20 minutes
Ages: 10 and up

Choose one player from each team to hold the pool noodle (these work well and are very safe). The players holding the noodle are neutral and become the goal. They run throughout the game area while trying to keep the noodle as straight as possible. Play as any small-sided game, except that both teams are trying to score on the same (moving) goal. A goal may be scored from either side of the noodle, and the team must have possession to score. You may want to change the players holding the noodle after every goal.

82. Wink

Purpose: To improve leg strength.

Number of Players: 9 to 11
Equipment: 4 or 5 balls (1 per pair)
Time: 5 to 10 minutes
Ages: 10 and up

Form a circle 10 yards in diameter. Players are in pairs, except for one player, who is in the middle of the circle without a ball. (If there is an even number of players, you can be the player in the middle.) One partner from each pair (the offensive player) has the ball and stands facing the center of the circle while her partner (the defensive player) stands behind her. All players are looking at the player in the middle. The player in the middle looks around the circle and winks at an offensive player. That offen-

sive player immediately begins to dribble toward the winker. Her partner, the defensive player, tries to prevent the offensive player from dribbling across the circle by grabbing her around the waist. The offensive player has until the count of ten to reach the winker. If the offensive player makes it, the defensive player becomes the new winker. If the defensive player keeps the offensive player from crossing the circle, the offensive and defensive players switch roles. The winker then winks at a new offensive player.

Safety note: Caution players to use common sense when exerting force to cross the circle.

83. Three-Touch Keep-Away

Purpose: To emphasize ball control, body posture, sense of touch, passing pace, and direction.

Number of Players: Two teams of 4 to 8 players each
Equipment: 1 ball, 4 cones
Time: 8 to 10 minutes
Ages: 12 and up

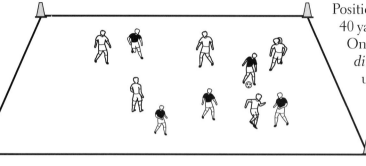

Position the teams in a playing area 30 to 40 yards wide and 40 to 50 yards long. One team plays with a *three-touch condition*, meaning that each player must use one touch to receive the ball, one touch to prepare the ball, and the third touch to pass the ball. The three-touch team must try to keep their balls away from the other team, who has no conditions on touches. After a reasonable period of time, switch the conditions of the teams. If the three-touch team makes three complete passes, it counts as a goal. If the team with no restrictions completes six passes, award them a point.

84. Attacking and Defending Gates

Purpose: To improve dribbling under pressure, decision making, and creative problem solving.

Number of Players: All
Equipment: 1 ball per player on team A, 12 to 20 cones
Time: 10 to 12 minutes
Ages: 10 and up

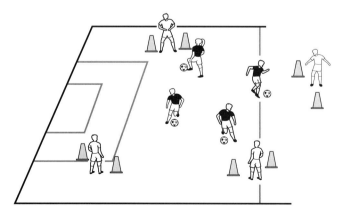

Divide the players into two teams: team A is the offensive team, and team B is the defensive team. Randomly place cones to create six to ten gates on half the field. The gates should be 3 yards wide. Each team A player takes on a team B player—they play one-on-one—and tries to play the ball through one of the gates. If a team B player wins the ball, she and the team A player switch roles. Play continues until time is up.

85. Outnumbered

Purpose: To develop the ability to maintain possession of the ball while under heavy pressure.

Number of Players: All, in groups of 3
Equipment: 1 ball per group
Time: 5 to 10 minutes
Ages: 10 and up

Have one player in each group try to maintain control of the ball while the other two players try to take it away. Once the ball is taken off the player, the player who wins it must try to maintain possession and the activity continues. Play 30-second intervals. The players who don't have the ball at the end of the interval must perform a simple task.

86. Soccer Chess

Purpose: To improve decision making, working in pairs, timing of runs, and wall passing.

Number of Players: 12 or more
Equipment: 4 balls, 4 cones
Time: 10 to 15 minutes
Ages: 11 and up

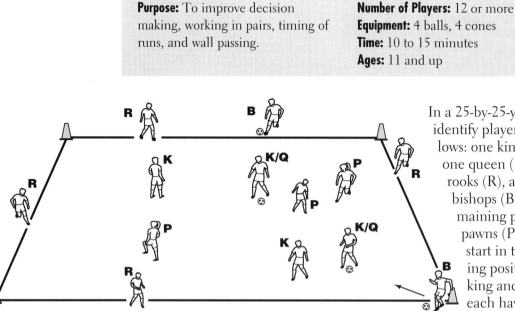

In a 25-by-25-yard grid, identify players as follows: one king, and one queen (K/Q), four rooks (R), and two bishops (B). The remaining players are pawns (P). Players start in the following positions: The king and queen each have a ball inside the square.

All pawns are also in the square but without balls. The four rooks are on the outside on each side and cannot come into the square. The two bishops are also on the outside, each with a ball, and they are allowed to enter the square.

The king and queen try to "knight" all of the pawns by hitting them with their balls through dribbling and short passing. Pawns run inside the square to try to avoid getting hit by the king or queen. The king and queen dribble anywhere in the area to try to hit the pawns. Pawns who have been hit become knights and place their hands on their hips to indicate that they have been knighted. A knight is stationary and can take only two or three steps in any one direction at a time. A knight may help the king and queen by acting as targets for one-touch wall passes to try to hit a pawn. The rooks also help the king and queen as one-touch wall players from the outside to assist in hitting a pawn. Again, knights and rooks can hit pawns from a one-touch pass.

The bishops, who each have a ball, dribble around the outside of the square. Their task is to change the knights back into pawns. To accomplish this, they must enter the square (board) from a corner and exit to the opposite corner. If during their running dribble they can tag a knight, the knight changes back into a pawn. If, however, the king or queen is able to hit a bishop with a ball, that bishop becomes a knight and can be freed only by the other bishop. The game is over when all of the pawns and bishops are knighted.

Play until all players are knighted or for a fixed time limit, counting the number of knights at the designated time. Allow players to play all of the roles.

CHAPTER 6

Target Games and Activities

Target activities provide opportunities for individuals or groups to play toward a target or goal. These activities direct players to a specific target or goal and thus offer the possibility of *transition* (switching from defense to offense) and attacking and defending a goal. Most of these activities will be more appropriate for players 10 years and older; however, several may be modified for younger players. These activities may also be structured according to level of intensity or complexity. Target activities still provide players and coaches opportunities for problem solving and creativity. Many of them may be modified by increasing or decreasing the playing space, the size and placement of the goals, the number of balls in play, and restrictions on types of movements or passing sequences.

87. Red Light, Green Light

Purpose: To develop listening skills and reaction time.

Number of Players: All
Equipment: 1 ball per player
Time: 5 to 10 minutes
Ages: 5 to 8

Establish two lines 20 to 25 yards apart. Players (each with a ball) start on one line while you (or a person designated It) stand on the opposite line. You (or It) face away from the players and call out "Green light!" Players then begin dribbling their balls toward the opposite line. When you call out "Red light!," players must freeze by placing their foot on top of their balls before you turn around and catch them still dribbling. Anyone caught must go back to the starting line. The first player to cross the end line takes your place (or becomes the new It), or can pick someone else who hasn't been It.

88. Open and Closed Gates

Purpose: To develop the ability to recognize when a goal is open and to quickly attack that goal.

Number of Players: 8 to 12
Equipment: 4 to 8 balls, 4 cones to mark playing area, 8 cones or flags to mark goals
Time: 5 to 10 minutes
Ages: All

Position the players in a 25-by-25-yard grid with one goal (gates) at each corner. Goals are approximately 5 yards wide and should be set up with two flags or cones at each corner. Place one player (the keeper) in each goal. You or a designated leader stands outside of the space. When the keepers are standing in the goal, the goal is considered closed and a ball cannot be played to that goal. When you point to a particular goal, that keeper either jumps outside of the goal, thus opening it, or jumps inside the goal, closing it.

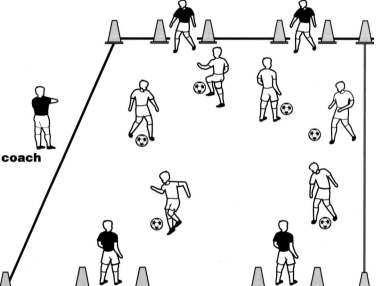

coach

The remaining four to eight players each have a ball and dribble inside the area. The game should begin with all goals closed (keepers standing inside the goal). When you point to a goal, that keeper jumps outside of the goal. Players with the balls try to dribble through or play a ball through to score in the open gate. If you point to the gate again before the ball is played through, the gate becomes closed and the goal does not count. Continue for several minutes randomly opening and closing gates. Switch players and add four new keepers.

Variation: For ages 8 and up, play the game in groups of two, three, or four. This adds the dimension of passing and cooperative play.

89. Balls Galore

Purpose: To introduce the concept of dribbling toward the goal.

Number of Players: Two teams of 4 to 6 players each
Equipment: 2 goals, several balls
Time: 10 to 15 minutes
Ages: 5 to 8 (but can be played with older players)

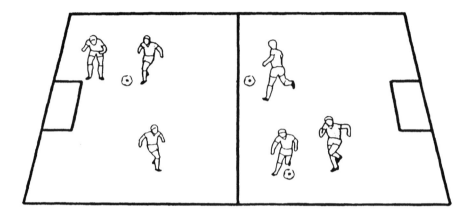

This small-sided game for younger players provides the opportunity for scoring many goals. Play a regular game to two goals using more than one ball. If your players always chase after one ball in a "beehive" fashion (in a clump around the ball), give them more "honey"! You may send balls into the field as they are played out-of-bounds. Try to keep at least three or four balls in the game at all times. When you run out of balls, ask players to run and collect them so you can start another round.

This game is a great opportunity to practice individual and group tactics. With gamelike pressure, players will break into "duels" of one-on-one, two-on-one, two-on-two, three-on-three, etc. Some players will stay in the back and defend, some players will chase (track) other players down the field, and some will take leadership roles.

TARGET GAMES AND ACTIVITIES

90. Tree Ball

Purpose: To help players to develop a game strategy.

Number of Players: All, in pairs
Equipment: 1 ball per pair, trees or other circle targets (created with flags or cones)
Time: 5 to 10 minutes
Ages: 8 and up

In this cat-and-mouse type of game, have all the pairs start approximately 30 yards from the designated trees or targets. (If there are no trees in your area, use flags or cones to create circle targets.) You can make a circuit, if you wish, or just use the trees that are near your playing area. For each pair, one partner strikes the ball toward the tree. Wherever the ball stops, the other partner strikes the ball. Play continues until one player in the pair hits the tree with a pass. The scoring player scores a point, and play continues with the other player striking the ball from where the ball rebounded off the tree. That pair can move on to the next tree or target, or begin a new round at this tree. Play using a time limit or a designated number of points.

91. Tree Ball Golf

Purpose: To improve passing accuracy.

Number of Players: All
Equipment: 1 ball per player, trees or other circle targets (created with flags or cones)
Time: 10 to 15 minutes
Ages: 8 and up

If you have trees in your area, use them as golf holes (hitting the trunk counts). (If there are no trees in your area, use flags or cones to create circle targets.) Start the players on the circuit. As in regular golf, the player who takes the fewest number of shots to hit each tree or target wins the "hole." This is a good cooldown activity.

Variation: Players can use a shot to hit an opponent's ball, potentially moving the opponent farther from the hole. The player who hit the opponent's ball away then gets another shot.

92. Soccer Golf

Purpose: To improve passing accuracy.	**Number of Players:** All **Equipment:** 1 ball per player **Time:** 5 to 10 minutes **Ages:** 8 and up

Select several objects (targets) around your training area and number them as holes on a golf course. You can designate, for example, goal posts, side netting, trash cans, trees, flags, telephone poles, bleachers, and so on. The only criteria is that it must be a safe area.

After you show players the course, players proceed one after another through the course, keeping their own scores. Each touch of the ball counts as a stroke. Consider establishing par for the course; that is, depending on the difficulty of a "hole," establish the average number of shots (three, four, or five) it should take players to hit the target. This is a good cooldown activity.

93. Many Goals

Purpose: To improve dribbling, passing to the feet, and team possession.	**Number of Players:** Two teams of 4 to 8 players each **Equipment:** 1 ball, 6 to 8 cones **Time:** 10 to 20 minutes **Ages:** 8 and up

Use cones to randomly set up three or four goals 3 yards apart in a half field. In this small-sided game, the team in possession tries to score by passing the ball through a goal to a teammate. A goal counts only if the scoring team keeps possession. Both teams play to the same goals.

TARGET GAMES AND ACTIVITIES

94. Bridge Passing

Purpose: To develop passing accuracy.

Number of Players: All, in pairs
Equipment: 1 ball per pair
Time: 5 to 10 minutes
Ages: 8 and up

Have partners stand approximately 10 yards apart. The partner without the ball stands with his legs apart as the goal or target. The player with the ball begins by trying to pass the ball between his partner's legs. The goal player does not move until the ball either goes through or misses the goal. At the moment the ball goes through or misses, the goal player quickly turns and sprints after the ball. After controlling the ball, the retrieving player turns and attempts to pass to the other player, who is now the goal. Players work together and also compete to see how far apart they can get and still score goals. Play for a designated time or until a player scores 10 points.

Encourage players to turn quickly and prepare the ball for the next pass to goal. Play should be continuous, not a stop-and-go or dead-ball activity. Have players try to keep the ball rolling at all times.

95. Edge of the World

Purpose: To introduce the concepts of ball pace (speed) and accuracy.

Number of Players: All
Equipment: 1 ball per player
Time: 3 to 5 minutes
Ages: 5 to 8

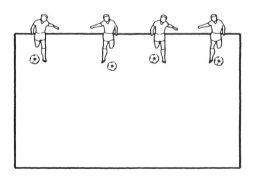

Starting at the end of the field in the penalty area, have each player pass her ball to the 18-yard line. Players run after their own balls and control them before they fall off the "edge of the world" (goes over the 18-yard line). Players may strike their balls only once when passing. Challenge players to get their balls as close to the line as they can without going over it.

This is a good warm-up or cooldown activity. It is self-pacing and allows the player to take safe risks.

96. Crows and Cranes

Purpose: To develop passing with the inside of the foot.

Number of Players: Two teams of 6 to 10 players each

Equipment: 6 to 10 balls, 4 cones or flags

Time: Until all players are on the same team

Ages: 8 and up

Use cones or flags to mark two end lines 40 to 60 yards apart. Have two lines of players face each other with an end line 20 to 30 yards away from each group. Place the balls in a line between the two teams. Stand at the end between the two lines of facing players. Designate one team the "Crows" and the other the "Cranes." When you call out either "Crows" or "Cranes," the team whose name was called tries to pass or dribble the balls to hit the other team. The team not called turns and sprints toward their own end line. If they cross the line without being hit, they go back to the center for the next round. Players who were hit join that team and assume their name.

The game is played until all players are on the same team. Who wins? Everyone!

97. Beehive Breakup

Purpose: To introduce moving off or away from the ball.

Number of Players: Two teams of 6 to 9 players each
Equipment: 1 ball, 2 goals, 12 cones
Time: 10 to 20 minutes
Ages: 8 and up

This small-sided game is played on a half field. Place cones evenly on the sides and end line around the field. Play as a normal game but immediately following each pass, have the passing player run and touch the nearest or farthest cone and then run back to the ball. You decide which distance to use during the game.

This is a great game for reducing the "beehive" effect of players bunching around the ball. It also provides the opportunity for equal participation, particularly if you have a few players who have a tendency to dominate play.

98. Get Outta Here

Purpose: To improve dribbling, short passing, receiving, quickness, sprinting, endurance, concentration, and teamwork.

Number of Players: 6 to 10, in pairs
Equipment: 6 to 10 balls, 4 cones to mark playing area, 4 cones or flags to mark goals
Time: 10 minutes
Ages: 8 and up

The name of this activity may sound a bit harsh, but it's one of the activities players seem to enjoy the most. Create a 20-by-40-yard grid with two goals. Stand at the middle of the field on one of the sidelines. All of the available balls should be placed at your feet. (This is absolutely necessary to keep the activity moving.)

To start the game, divide the players into two groups. The groups then line up on either side of you at the middle of the field. Play a ball onto the field without giving any spoken cues, such as "ready, get set, go" or "play." The idea is to see which players are perceptive enough to know that the game is on when there is a ball on the field. Two pairs (one from each team) are on the field at any one time.

Now the fun part begins. When a ball goes out-of-bounds, shout "Get outta here!" At this point, the pairs on the field must run off the field and go to the end of their team's line while, at the same time, the next pairs from each team race onto the field and start to play. Play one of the balls at your feet into the game so you can pass a ball to a player who hasn't had a lot of touches or into an open space to reduce bunching. If a goal is scored, yell "Get outta here!," and the pair who was scored on leaves the field while the scoring pair stays on the field, ready for more action.

When you have run out of balls, stop the game and have *all* of the players run to get all the balls back to you so play can resume.

TARGET GAMES AND ACTIVITIES

99. Gladiator Ball

Purpose: To encourage dribbling to penetrate, passing in small spaces, shooting accurately, and receiving balls in small spaces.

Number of Players: Two teams of 3 to 6 players each, depending on the age group (5- and 6-year-olds should not have more than 4 players per team)
Equipment: 1 ball per player, 4 cones to mark playing area, 4 cones or flags to mark goals
Time: 1-minute intervals
Ages: All

Create a playing area 20 to 30 yards wide and 30 to 40 yards long. Use flags or cones to mark two goals. There are no goalkeepers. Each player starts with a ball on her side of the field. On your signal, players try to score as many goals as they can in 1 minute. Once a ball goes in the goal or out-of-bounds, it cannot be put back into play. A player who loses a ball may receive a pass from a teammate or try to tackle a ball from the other team. After 1 minute, count the number of goals and then reset the game for another round.

100. Four-Corner Capture

| **Purpose:** To encourage small-group problem solving. | **Number of Players:** 8 to 16, in four groups
Equipment: 1 ball per player, 16 cones
Time: 10 to 15 minutes
Ages: 8 and up |

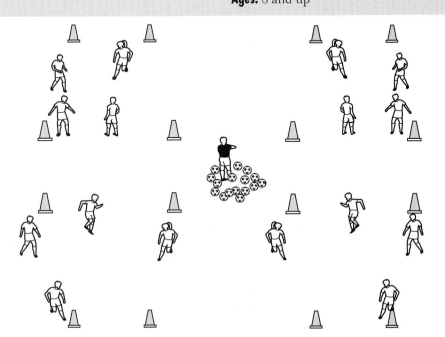

Create a 40-by-40-yard grid. In each corner, set up four cones in a 3-yard square. Each square has the same number of players. The activity can last 30, 60, or 90 seconds per round.

On your signal, players from each group run into the middle of the field to get a ball and dribble it back to their square. The first group who gets one more ball in their square than the number of players in the group scores 1 point. This can happen because players are allowed to "steal" balls from other squares. Allow only the use of soccer techniques to maintain possession of the balls in the square. No hand-to-hand combat, football blocking, tripping, or holding is permitted. Players have to solve the problem of maintaining possession of the balls in their square while other players in their group go to other squares and launch "sneak attacks." Do not allow any defending or passing at first.

Variations: After a few rounds, allow players to defend, meaning they can attempt to take balls away from other players as well as from the squares. After a few more rounds, allow players to pass balls to a square but do not allow defending or intercepting passes. Finally, allow players to dribble, pass, defend, and intercept balls, which is almost like a game.

101. Playing to Four Targets

Purpose: To encourage changing the point of attack and to develop small-group tactics.

Number of Players: Two teams of 4 to 8 players each
Equipment: 1 ball, 4 cones to mark playing area, 8 flags to mark goals
Time: 10 to 20 minutes
Ages: 8 and up

The field should be appropriately sized for the number of players, ranging from 20 by 30 yards to a half field. Use the flags to mark four goals, either on each corner or on each side of the field. Each team must defend and attack two goals. Play either with or without goalkeepers. If you play with goalkeepers, then a team's goalkeeper must defend both of her team's goals.

Variation: Have players play to a teammate who runs into one of the goals the team is attacking. If the teammate receives the ball cleanly, a goal is scored and the team retains possession to attack the other goals. No goalkeepers are used in this variation.

102. Score on the End Line

Purpose: To encourage small-group tactics of pressure, coverage (support), and balance while developing teamwork and group problem solving.

Number of Players: Two teams of 3 to 7 players each
Equipment: 1 ball, 4 cones
Time: 5 to 10 minutes
Ages: 9 and up

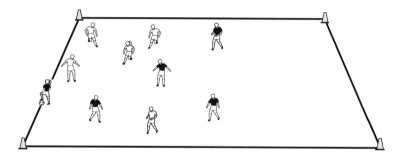

Create a field appropriately sized for the number of players, ranging from 20 by 30 yards to a half field. Two teams play a normal soccer game, but the only way to score is to stop the ball along the opponent's end line.

Variation: Have the scoring team keep the ball and immediately attack the other end line.

103. Soccer Volleyball

Purpose: To improve receiving air balls, volleys, and to improve touch (ball feel) by encouraging quick reaction, balance, and ball placement.

Number of Players: Two teams of 2 to 4 players each
Equipment: 1 ball, 4 flags or cones to mark playing area, 2 flags or cones to mark net
Time: 10 to 20 minutes
Ages: 10 and up

Create a space that looks like a volleyball court on your field, appropriately sized for the number of players you have and their skill level. For example, if you have four players on each team, use a 20-by-20-yard grid; with five players per team, use a 25-by-25-yard grid. Use two flags or cones to mark the net. To score, a ball needs only to cross an imaginary midline in the air. Players use only soccer skills (no hands). Otherwise the game is played and scored as in volleyball. The ball is put into play through a punt from the end line. Allow each team to have one bounce, or limit the number of touches.

This game can be used as a training activity when you must have at least two touches per side.

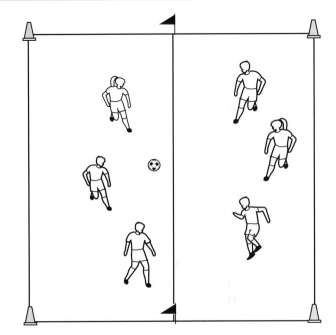

104. Soccer Tennis

Purpose: To improve touch and ballhandling abilities.

Number of Players: All, in groups of 4 divided into pairs
Equipment: 1 ball per group, 4 cones, 1 midline marker
Time: Until one team gets 10 points
Ages: 10 and up

Using four cones, set up a 10-by-20-yard space. Use cones, flags, or a small bench as a marker for the midline. Each pair plays in a 10-by-10-yard box like in tennis. Use tennis or volleyball scoring but permit only soccer skills. The serving team begins by punting the ball into their opponent's box. The ball can bounce only once per side. The receiving team can have an unlimited number of touches on their side as long as the ball doesn't hit the ground more than once. The ball is played back and forth until someone misses or the ball goes out-of-bounds. A ball must be in the air when it crosses the imaginary net.

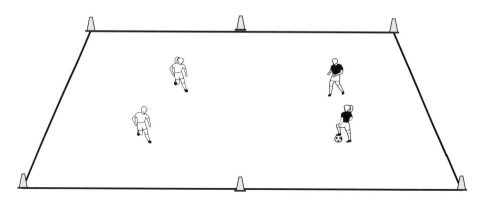

105. Two-on-One

Purpose: To develop two-player combinations to beat defenders (get the ball behind them).

Number of Players: All, in groups of 4
Equipment: 1 ball, 4 cones to mark playing area, 4 cones or flags to mark goals
Time: 10 to 15 minutes
Ages: 9 and up

Create a grid 10 to 15 yards wide by 20 to 25 yards long with a goal on each end line. Play two-on-one with the second defender acting as the goalkeeper. Once a goal is scored, or when the ball is stopped or goes over the end line, the goalkeeper/defender comes onto the field and joins his partner. One player from the new defending team then must drop back to defend the goal. The team in possession of the ball always has both players on the field, while the defending team may have only one player on the field. There is always a two-on-one situation on the field.

Examples of two-player combinations are wall passes, overlaps, and takeovers. In *wall passes*, the passing player plays a ball to a teammate, who immediately (with only one touch—similar to playing it off a wall) plays it behind the defender and back to the first passing player. *Overlaps* occur when one player plays the ball to a teammate, then runs around and past the teammate to receive the return pass, in order to beat the defender. Thus the first player is overlapping the player he passed to. *Takeovers* occur when one player dribbles the ball toward a teammate, fakes leaving the ball to deceive the defender, and then keeps it.

106. Numbers Shoot

Purpose: To improve communication, movement off the ball, and getting players into scoring situations.

Number of Players: Two teams of 4 to 8 players each
Equipment: 1 ball, 4 cones to mark playing area, 4 flags or cones to mark goals
Time: 10 to 20 minutes
Ages: 11 and up

Create a playing area with the cones, and mark a goal on each end line. The playing area should be appropriate for the number of players, ranging from 20 by 30 yards to a half field. Give each player a number (e.g., if playing five-on-five, team members would be numbered 1 to 5). Whenever you call out a number, that is the only player who may shoot. Challenge players to receive the ball and be in shooting position in fewer than four passes once their name is called.

107. Attack the Crabs

Purpose: To develop the ability to dribble through a maze of players.

Number of Players: All, in two teams of equal number
Equipment: 1 ball per player on team A, 1 goal
Time: 1-minute intervals
Ages: 10 and up

Members of team B are sitting down, randomly spaced inside the 18-yard box but not in the 6-yard box. These are the crab players. Team A players, each with a ball, stand at the 18-yard line. On your signal, team A players attempt to dribble through the maze of crab players. Once team A players get through the maze and enter the 6-yard goal box under control, they shoot at the goal, pick up their balls, and start again. Team A tries to score as many goals as possible in 1 minute. Team B players are permitted to move but must remain in the crab position. They attempt to kick team A's balls out-of-bounds. When a ball is kicked away, the team A player runs after it and starts over at the 18-yard line.

Keep track of the time and the total number of goals scored. At the end of 1 minute, teams reverse roles. Emphasize dribbling through the crabs and crossing the 6-yard line before shooting on the goal.

108. Rock, Scissors, Paper

Purpose: To develop passing with the inside of the foot.

Number of Players: Two teams of 6 to 10 players each
Equipment: 6 to 10 balls
Time: Until all players are on the same team
Ages: 10 and up

Position two lines of players facing each other with an end line 20 to 30 yards away from each group. Place the balls in a line between the two teams and stand at the end between the two lines of facing players.

Players use the following familiar symbols from the Rock, Scissors, Paper game: a clenched fist for "rock"; the first two fingers apart for "scissors"; and an open palm facing up for "paper." The rules are that rock dulls scissors (rock wins); scissors cuts paper (scissors wins); and paper covers rock (paper wins). Each team forms a huddle and decides which symbol to throw. All players on the same team must throw the same symbol (it helps to have a second choice in case both teams choose the same symbol). When you call, "Rock-scissors-paper, 1, 2, 3, throw!," both teams immediately show their symbol; the team whose symbol wins tries to pass or dribble the balls to hit the other team. The losing team turns and sprints toward their own end line. If they cross the line before being hit, they go back to the center for the next round. Players who were hit join that team. Players form a new huddle and select new symbols.

Play the game until all players are on the same team. Who wins? Again, everyone!

109. Soccer Baseball

Purpose: To work on team running, passing, and shooting techniques.

Number of Players: All, in two teams of equal number
Equipment: 1 ball, 1 goal, 4 cones to mark bases
Time: 15 to 20 minutes
Ages: 10 and up

Use cones to mark out three bases and home plate, starting from the goal. Home plate is to the left of the goal where the 6-yard line intersects the end line. The batter stands to the right of the goal to receive the pitch. Spacing the bases will require a trial-and-error approach to find the most appropriate distance.

Play the game like baseball, with a pitcher and fielding players, except for the following rule changes.

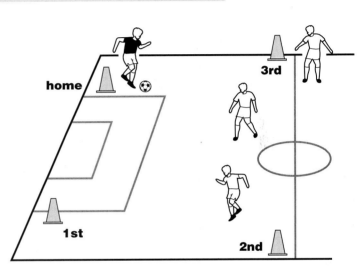

- Don't keep track of outs; the inning is over when everyone has kicked.
- The kicking player must run around and touch all of the bases. The player cannot stop at any of the bases; the run ends with either an out or a run scored.
- The fielding team receives the kick and, through passing and shooting, tries to kick the ball into the goal before the runner crosses home plate to get the runner out. There are no goalkeepers.

Play as many innings as you like. This is a fun activity that works on communication and teamwork. Depending on your players' skill level, you may want them to try playing one, two, or three touches and/or to require that the goal shot cross the goal line in the air.

TARGET GAMES AND ACTIVITIES

110. Group One-on-One to Goal

Purpose: To develop the ability to attack and defend one-on-one.

Number of Players: All, in pairs
Equipment: 1 ball per pair, 1 goal
Time: 5 to 15 minutes
Ages: 10 and up

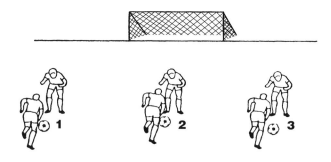

In each pair, one player defends and one player attacks. Position the pairs, each with a ball, at midfield, stretched across the field.

The attacker and defender should be no more than 2 yards apart with the attacker facing the goal and the defender facing the attacker. Everyone is in a one-on-one position. Number each pair in sequence starting with number 1.

To begin, all attackers move their balls at the midfield line with the defenders applying token pressure. The attackers are not trying to beat the defenders at this time, but all partners are in motion in a shadow-boxing type of activity. Then call out a pair's number. This is the signal for that attacker to attempt to beat his defender and go to the goal. The defender tries to prevent penetration and win the ball. Defenders track the attackers until a shot is taken. After each attack to the goal, players switch roles. To keep the activity moving, call another number when one group is halfway to the goal. This activity is a great alternative to a typical drill where a line of forwards goes against a line of defenders, and most of the players must wait to take a turn.

Variation: To make things more competitive, have an attacker who scores remain an attacker or have a defender who wins the ball become the attacker.

111. Junkyard Soccer

Purpose: To develop the ability to play balls quickly out of one's half of the field.

Number of Players: All, in two teams of equal number
Equipment: 1 ball per player
Time: 5 to 10 minutes
Ages: 10 and up

This game can be played on a full field with one team on each half. Create a neutral zone in the middle of the field (5 yards into each half).

On your signal, both teams begin to kick their balls to the other side. The objective is to be the first team to kick the balls quickly enough to get all of them on one side (like in a hot-potato or pepper game). When all the balls from one team are on one side, award that team a point and start again. To prevent players from being hit by balls played close or balls they don't see, no one is allowed in the neutral zone. If a ball stops in the neutral zone, you should run through quickly and kick it back into play. The game can also be played with a time limit, in which the team with the least number of balls on their side wins the round.

112. Team Circuit Training

Purpose: To work on specific dribbling, passing, receiving, and shooting techniques.

Number of Players: All
Equipment: 12 balls, 8 to 10 cones to mark stations, 2 goals (for the shooting station)
Time: 10 to 20 minutes
Ages: 10 and up

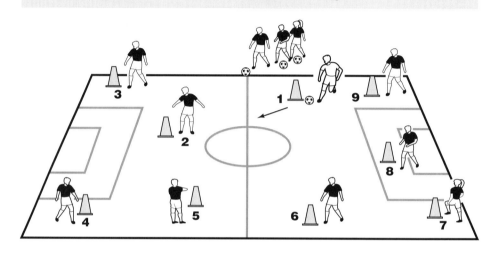

Use the cones to set up 8 to 10 different stations (areas of the field), numbered sequentially, throughout a full field. This forms the circuit. Stations should include dribbling, passing to targets, receiving, and shooting. To start, place one player without a ball at each station. All other players should get a ball and form a line at station 1. The first player (player 1) plays her ball to the player at station 2 and sprints to station 2. The player at station 2 (player 2) receives the ball and plays it to the player at station 3. Player 2 then sprints to station 3. The circuit continues in this manner, with players sprinting following their plays and players playing the balls to the next station.

When the first ball reaches station 3 or 4, start a new ball and player. Once the circuit gets going, you should have several balls moving on the circuit at the same time. This speeds up the activity as well as decreases the preparation time players have to receive and play the ball to the next station.

113. Heads Up

Purpose: To learn to head the ball while moving with control and power while under pressure.

Number of Players: All

Equipment: 1 ball, 4 cones or flags, 2 goals (for variation)

Time: 10 to 12 minutes

Ages: 10 and up

Position two teams in 40-by-50-yard grid. Players may touch the ball with only their hands and their heads. A team maintains possession by throwing (hand passing) to a teammate and earns points when a ball passed to a teammate is successfully headed from the receiving player to another teammate. Players must be moving to earn team points. Play in small numbers at first for younger players (e.g., 10-year-olds).

Variation: Add a goal to each end of the playing area. A goal scored off a head is worth 3 points, and each head pass during play is worth 1 point.

114. Team Four-on-Two

Purpose: To improve short and long passing skills and changing the point of attack.

Number of Players: Three teams of 6 players each
Equipment: 1 ball per team, 12 cones
Time: 10 to 15 minutes
Ages: 10 and up

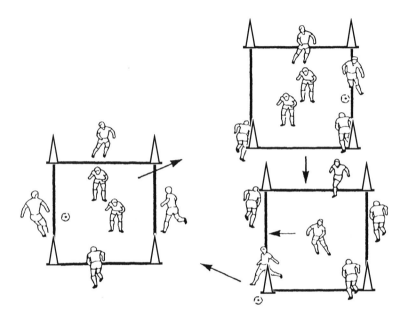

Set up three 10-by-15-yard grids that are 20 to 30 yards apart in a triangle. Within each team, players should have a permanent partner. (It is possible for one partner to be in the middle and one to be on the outside.) Play begins with each team playing four-on-two keep-away within their area. If the players in the middle get or touch their group's ball, those players come out. After that first exchange, the players who have been in the longest come out.

On your signal, in each group the player in possession of the ball plays it to the next grid. All passes should go in a clockwise or counterclockwise movement. The passer and his partner then sprint to the grid where the ball was played. These two new players to the grid begin in the middle as the defenders. Essentially, each team has two players leaving and two new players joining the grid. The four players receiving the ball from the long passes immediately begin passing the ball between them. This continues, with player changes in the grid, until you blow the whistle again for another change.

115. Throw-Receive-Catch (T-R-C)

Purpose: To develop the ability to receive air balls with the chest and thighs.

Number of Players: All, in two teams of equal number
Equipment: 1 ball, 2 goals
Time: 15 to 25 minutes
Ages: 10 and up

Place two goals on the end lines of a half or full field. Begin play by giving one team the ball. Players must follow the throw-receive-catch sequence. That is, one teammate throws the ball to a second teammate, who controls it with a no-hands, body-part reception and then catches it. Players in possession of the ball may take only three steps before they must throw it to a teammate, who then repeats the sequence. The object is to move the ball down the field toward the goal. Goals are scored by heading a ball after a toss. The defending team can gain possession only

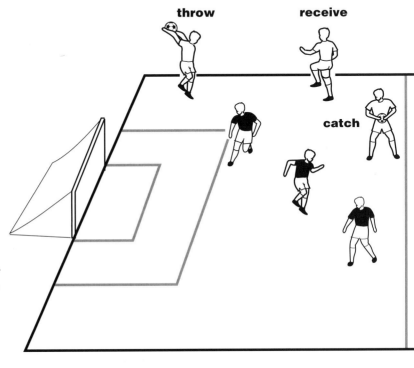

through intercepting (catching) a toss in the air. Once the defending team has the ball, the team must follow the same T-R-C sequence while moving down the field toward the goal. A dropped ball can go to the other team or you can allow the player who dropped it to pick it up and continue play.

If players are having difficulty moving the ball or scoring, count each successful sequence as a point, and make 10 points equal to a goal.

116. Box-on-Box Shooting

Purpose: To develop a shooting mentality while outnumbered.

Number of Players: Two teams of 4 players each
Equipment: Several balls, 2 large goals
Time: 10 to 20 minutes
Ages: 10 and up

Play the game in areas the size of two penalty boxes, with the 18-yard line as the dividing line. Place goals at each end. Position one offensive player (the forward) with three defensive players, thus creating a three-on-one situation. Place goalkeepers in each goal.

Begin by serving a ball to one side. If the three defenders win the ball, they play quick passes to each other so that their forward on the other side of the field can get free to receive the ball. They should play the ball to their forward as quickly as possible. When the three defenders players have the ball, the forward from the other team tries to steal the ball to score. If a defensive player has an opportunity to shoot, she can also try to score from her defensive position.

As soon as a ball is played out-of-bounds, serve another ball. Play 2- to 3-minute rounds; then rotate teams and allow each player to become the forward.

Variation: After the players get into a rhythm of the game, allow one defensive player to make a run into the attack when the forward from the defending team has the ball. This player may have limited or unlimited touches but must return after that particular play is over.

117. Triangle Goal

Purpose: To develop dribbling, passing, heading, receiving, and shooting skills while improving cardiovascular endurance.

Number of Players: Two teams of 6 to 9 players each
Equipment: 1 ball, 3 cones or flags
Time: 10 to 20 minutes
Ages: 10 and up

Place the three cones or flags in the center of your playing space to create a triangle goal with each side approximately 6 to 8 yards apart. Outside boundaries are not that important, unless your space presents safety concerns. The defending team places three players in the triangle (one per side), who act as goalkeepers for their side. The remaining players play with three players down on the field against the attacking team, either six-on-three or nine-on-six. If a goal is scored, the attacking team retains possession. If the defending team wins the ball on the field or one of the three goalkeepers makes a stop, three players from the new defending team must quickly take goalkeeping positions in the triangle.

118. Team in the Middle

Purpose: To encourage players to maintain possession and to help them identify when to play a forward or penetrating pass.

Number of Players: Three teams of 4 to 6 players each
Equipment: 1 ball, 4 cones
Time: 10 to 20 minutes
Ages: 10 and up

Create a small-sided field divided into three 20-by-30-yard zones. Size may vary depending on the size and ability level of your players. The game starts with a team in each zone. The two end teams play keep-away with the team in the middle. Players are not allowed to leave their zone. Every time a team plays through the middle zone without the ball being intercepted, the passing team receives a point. If the passing team plays the ball out-of-bounds or it is intercepted, they move into the middle. Encourage the team in possession to pass the ball to create a clear path to the other end. Play for a designated time or until a team earns 10 points.

Variation: Permit one player from the middle team to enter the end zone to put more pressure on the ball. If that player wins the ball there, his team moves out of the middle.

119. Team Knockout to Goal

Purpose: To introduce the concepts of direct and indirect play.

Number of Players: Two teams of 6 to 9 players each
Equipment: 1 ball per player on team B, 1 goal
Time: Depends on ability and interest level
Ages: 10 and up

This game is similar to Team Knockout (#75). Position the two teams on a half field. Team B is on the field, and each player has a ball. Team A players position themselves anywhere along the sidelines without balls. On your signal, you start the clock and team A runs on to the field and attempts to intercept any of team B's balls and score. Team B players who have had their balls taken away can help other team members by getting into position to receive a pass, regain their balls, or defend the goal. The objective is to see how long team B can keep at least one ball in play or how many goals team A can score. Stop the clock when the last ball is out-of-bounds or in the goal. Then switch roles and see if team A can beat team B's time.

This is an excellent activity for improving communication and the concept of direct play (team A), and working on maintaining possession and the concept of indirect play (team B).

120. Star Trek

Purpose: To emphasize midfield preparation and possession.

Number of Players: Three teams of 3 to 7 players each
Equipment: 1 ball
Time: 15 to 30 minutes
Ages: 10 and up

Divide a full field into equal thirds designated the defensive, midfield, and attacking thirds. Position one team in each third. The middle third is called the neutral zone, and the team in that zone gets the ball.

The middle team passes the ball in their zone to prepare an attack against one of the teams in either end zone. The middle team enters one end zone to score a goal while the team in the other end zone is resting. Only the team in possession of the ball may be in the neutral zone. If the attacking team scores, they keep the ball, return to the neutral zone, and prepare an attack against the resting team. If the defense wins the ball, they enter the neutral zone and attack the resting team. The former attacking team must enter the vacated end zone and rest.

Each team keeps track of its own score. Encourage players to use one- and two-touch passing in the neutral zone, to change the point of attack, and to get in advance of the ball by running into attacking spaces to receive a pass from the midfield or neutral zone.

121. All Up and Back

Purpose: To introduce the concept of total team movement.

Number of Players: Two teams of 5 to 11 players each
Equipment: 1 ball, 2 goals
Time: 20 to 30 minutes
Ages: 10 and up

Play on a half or full field with two goals. To get your team to move together, impose the condition that a goal counts only if *all* of the attacking team players (except the goal-keepers) are on the offensive half of the field. Conversely, when the team loses the ball, *all* defending players are expected to run back into their own half.

This is a very good transition game that helps minimize the gaps between defenders, midfielders, and forwards. If you want to really make it interesting, also require that the goalkeeper be on the attacking half for a goal to count.

122. The Crossing Game

Purpose: To improve communication and develop players' ability to change the point of attack through crossing.

Number of Players: Two teams of 3 to 8 players each
Equipment: 1 ball, 4 cones to mark play-ing area, 4 cones or flags to mark goals
Time: 10 to 20 minutes
Ages: 10 and up

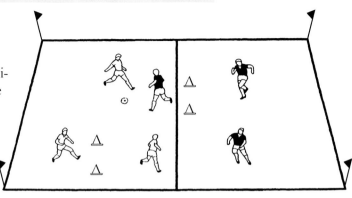

Play this small-sided game in a 30-by-40-yard area (depending on the team size, it could be larger). Use cones or flags to position two goals on the field as shown in the diagram. This activity is interesting be-cause the goals are not directly opposite each other but are staggered right and left. This forces players to change the point of the attack by making crosses to score. You may want to allow teams to score on both sides of the goal and have your goalkeeper defend both sides.

This is a great transition and finishing small-sided game that will improve how quickly players create an attack or transition to defense.

123. North-South-East-West

Purpose: To improve changing of direction when attacking and defending.

Number of Players: Two teams of 5 to 9 players each
Equipment: 1 ball
Time: 10 to 15 minutes
Ages: 10 and up

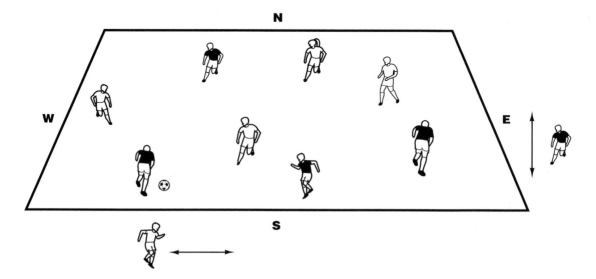

Play on a half field or a rectangular area appropriately sized for the age and number of players. One team will always be attacking in a north-south direction, while the other team will always attack in an east-west direction. A goal is scored when the attacking team can play a ball to a teammate along their goal lines, which are the end lines for the east-west team and the sidelines for the north-south team. Once a goal is scored, play immediately continues to the opposite end. The team that scores keeps the ball. As soon as the defending team wins the ball, they change direction and go toward the end line they choose. This allows all players to be part of both attacking and defending sequences.

124. Doubleheader

Purpose: To improve concentration, heading to the goal, and working in pairs.

Number of Players: 4, in pairs
Equipment: 1 ball, 4 cones or flags to mark playing area, 4 flags to mark goals
Time: 10 to 15 minutes
Ages: 11 and up

Create 10-by-20-yard grid with two goals that are 8 yards apart. Only heading is allowed. Position one pair in the middle and the other pair between the flags on their goal line and acting as goalkeepers. Play begins when one partner of the attacking pair tosses the ball to his partner, who must head the ball. Both players proceed toward their opponent's goal while heading the ball back and forth and to try to score a goal with a header (hands cannot touch the ball). If the ball hits the ground, the ball is dead and the players must run back to their goal while the players who were goalkeepers run out, pick up the ball, and begin heading it back and forth to the opposite goal.

Play for several minutes or set an objective (e.g., the first team to score three goals). Goalkeepers cannot use their hands or leave the goal line.

125. Ready, Aim, Fire!

Purpose: To emphasize playing with the head up and shooting while under of time, space, and offensive pressure.

Number of Players: Two teams of 4 or 5 players each, plus 2 goalkeepers
Equipment: 6 to 10 balls, 2 flags or cones to mark smaller goal, 1 larger goal
Time: 10 to 20 minutes
Ages: 12 and up

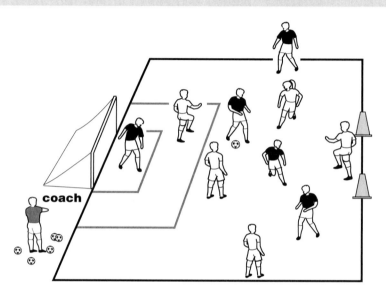

Divide the players into two teams plus goalkeepers. Place the large goal on one side of the penalty box and use the two flags or cones to set up a second goal on the other side of the penalty box. Because the game is played in the penalty box, players are allowed only two touches to score. You should have all of the balls at your feet and put them into play as the game ball goes out-of-bounds. Players may pass, but *all* players can have only two touches—one touch to receive, one touch to shoot or pass.

APPENDIX: Official Soccer Field Dimensions

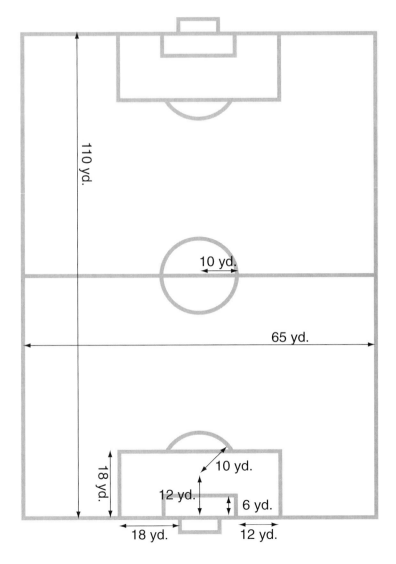

Skills Index

To aid in your practice planning, we've organized the activities by the skill they work on.

Note: Since all the activities emphasize keeping kids moving, they'll be improving their physical fitness (and having fun at the same time). However, the final problem solution in the Troubleshooting Chart on pages 31–33 suggests some activities that have a stronger fitness component.

Index

Acknowledgments

We would like to thank the U.S. Youth Soccer Association (USYSA), the National Soccer Coaches Association of America (NSCAA), and the U.S. Soccer Federation for providing the professional opportunities to develop our teaching methods. In addition, our respective institutions, Idaho Youth Soccer Association and Xavier University, have been most supportive of our work.

We would also like to express our appreciation to all of the youth coaches who have attended our various coaching education programs throughout the years.

A special thank-you to Kwik Goal for generously providing the equipment used in the photo shoot for this book.

And finally, much gratitude goes to Dr. Marianne Torbert, professor and director of the Leonard Gordon Institute for Human Growth Through Play at Temple University, whose work was a seed in the development in our ideas.

Tom Fleck and Ron Quinn

About the Authors

Tom Fleck is an authority on youth soccer development and education in the United States. He holds a doctorate in education from Lehigh University and is a certified elementary educator. He is currently the director of coaching and player development for the Idaho Youth Soccer Association and a member of the U.S. Youth Soccer Association Coaching Committee. Previously Dr. Fleck was the director of coaching for the Florida State Youth Association for thirteen years. His background also includes positions as the first U.S. Youth Soccer Coordinator, general manager of the Philadelphia Fury of the North American Soccer League, and head soccer coach and principal of the Centennial School at Lehigh University.

Dr. Fleck is a past president of the NSCAA, a senior member of the U.S. Soccer National Coaching Staff, and a technical advisor to FIFA (soccer's world governing body). He is the coauthor of the USYSA Parent/Coach Series of coaching booklets. In 1997 he received the first National Soccer Coaches Association of America Bill Jefferies Award for dedication and commitment to youth soccer.

Ron Quinn is an associate professor and director of the sport studies program at Xavier University, where he is also head coach of the women's soccer team. He holds a bachelor's degree in health and physical education and master and doctorate degrees in physical education and sport administration.

Dr. Quinn has been a teacher and coach for twenty-six years at all levels—from elementary school to university physical education and youth to professional coaching. He has written extensively on youth soccer player development and coaching education and, along with Dr. Fleck, is an innovator in the area of youth soccer player development. They were instrumental in the design and development of the national and state youth coaching license programs for U.S. Soccer.

Dr. Quinn is a member of the U.S. Youth Soccer Association Coaching Committee and the U.S. Soccer Federation National Teaching Staff. He is also a member of the National Soccer Coaches Association, where he formerly held the position of nonresidential director for the NSCAA Coaching Academy.